In His Kingdom

Embarking on a Journey Through God's Life Changing Kingdom

Copyright © 2023 by Rosel Joy Bona

ISBN 978-0-6459399-0-3 (Paperback)

All rights reserved.

All Scripture quotations, unless otherwise indicated, are taken from the Holy Bible, New International Version®, NIV®. Copyright ©1973, 1978, 1984, 2011 by Biblica, Inc. Used by permission of Zondervan. All rights reserved worldwide. www.zondervan.com The "N.I.V." and "New International Version" are trademarks registered in the United States Patent and Trademark Office by Biblica, Inc.

All Scripture quotations, unless otherwise indicated, are taken from the Holy Bible, New International Reader's Version®, NIrV® Copyright © 1995, 1996, 1998, 2014 by Biblica, Inc. Used by permission of Zondervan. All rights reserved worldwide. www.zondervan.com The "NIrV" and "New International Reader's Version" are trademarks registered in the United States Patent and Trademark Office by Biblica, Inc.

All Scripture quotations, unless otherwise indicated, are taken from the Amplified Bible, Copyright © 1954, 1958, 1962, 1964, 1965, 1987 by The Lockman Foundation. They are used by permission.

Unless otherwise noted, all Scripture quotations are taken from the Holman Christian Standard Bible®, Copyright © 1999, 2000, 2002, 2003, 2009 by Holman Bible Publishers. Used with permission by Holman Bible Publishers, Nashville, Tennessee. All rights reserved.

Scripture taken from the New King James Version®. Copyright © 1982 by Thomas Nelson. Used by permission. All rights reserved.

"Scripture quotations taken from the (NASB®) New American Standard Bible®, Copyright © 1960, 1971, 1977, 1995, 2020 by The Lockman Foundation. Used by permission. All rights reserved. lockman.org"

Scripture quoted by permission. Quotations designated (N.E.T.) are from the N.E.T. Bible® copyright ©1996, 2019 by Biblical Studies Press, L.L.C. http://netbible.com. All rights reserved.

No portion of this book may be reproduced in any form without written permission from the publisher or author except as permitted by U.S. copyright law.

ROSEL JOY BONA

This publication is designed to provide accurate and authoritative information in regard to the subject matter covered. It is sold with the understanding that neither the author nor the publisher is engaged in rendering legal, investment, accounting or other professional services. While the publisher and author have used their best efforts in preparing this book, they make no representations or warranties with respect to the accuracy or completeness of the contents of this book and specifically disclaim any implied warranties of merchantability or fitness for a particular purpose. No warranty may be created or extended by sales representatives or written sales materials. The advice and strategies contained herein may not be suitable for your situation. You should consult with a professional when appropriate. Neither the publisher nor the author shall be liable for any loss of profit or any other commercial damages, including but not limited to special, incidental, consequential, personal, or other damages.

Book Cover designed by Rosel Joy Bona

First edition November 2023

IN
EMBARKING ON A JOURNEY
HIS
THROUGH GOD'S LIFE CHANGING
KINGDOM
WRITTEN BY
ROSEL JOY BONA

Contents

Preface	VII
Dedication	X
Introduction	XII
1. In His Kingdom Exploring the Call	1
2. In His Kingdom Heart Love, Compassion and Forgiveness	32
3. In His Kingdom Identity Discovering Our True Identity	51
4. In His Kingdom Values Living a Righteous Life in a World Filled with Turmoil	68
5. In His Kingdom Wisdom Seeking God's Guidance in Decision-making	85
6. In His Kingdom Power Accessing Supernatural Strength	105
7. In His Kingdom Stories Doors, Windows, Rope Holders, and Basket Cases.	118
8. In His Kingdom Provision Finding Comfort in God's Faithfulness	133

9.	In His Kingdom Purpose Uncovering and Fulfilling God's Unique Plan	143
10.	In His Kingdom Transformation Growing and Maturing in the Likeness of Christ	154
11.	In His Kingdom Warfare Standing Strong amidst Spiritual Challenges.	166
12.	In His Kingdom Hope Hope in God Promises	177
13.	In His Kingdom Expansion Sharing and Multiplication	188

Epilogue	202
Bibliography	205
About the Author	217

Preface

Sometimes in life, we experience moments of solitude where it feels like the world has turned its back on us. We bear the burden of betrayal from those we once held dear and trusted, investing our time and energy for their benefit. It is during these times that we often seek solace and inspiration in our passions. For me, I found comfort through writing during a challenging period, and it was during this journey that I felt guided by a higher power. God's whispers became my source of encouragement.

Being the pastor of Life Choice Church has been a privilege. Our congregation is vibrant and immersed in a spirited atmosphere. Love is expressed as our language, compassion serves as the currency we exchange with one another, and forgiveness echoes as our anthem. Aside from my duties, I also have the honour of overseeing churches in Africa and the Philippines as a global overseer. Every year, I make it a priority to visit these churches, hosting conferences for pastors and leaders while extending support to villages that are deserving of aid and encouragement. It is through these endeavours that I witness firsthand the divine movement within God's kingdom.

During my visits, pastors and community leaders often approached me, asking for recommendations on resources and websites to enhance their understanding of the kingdom. Although I wished to provide them with guidance, I humbly responded, "I am a servant like you seeking to witness the kingdom of God in the lives of others." Little did I realize that these encounters would lead me to a realization during a prayerful morning on December 29, 2017.

In a whisper, I heard God's voice saying, *"This year I will elevate you to higher places and position you like an eagle so that you can clearly see the true objective."* Initially, I couldn't fully grasp the meaning behind these words. However, as time passed by, it dawned on me that there were three books within my heart waiting to be written – including "In His Kingdom.". The mystery remained: how would I bring them into publication?

It was during a series of sermons about humility in His Kingdom that an unexpected consequence unfolded. One by one, my trusted key leaders started leaving the church without any explanation. Some even walked out during preaching sessions. This random act of betrayal left me feeling abandoned and deeply hurt, causing me to question the foundations on which our shared vision was built. During my moments, I turned to writing to find solace and inner strength. It became my refuge where I could rediscover the courage to rise again and again.

There were instances when I seriously considered giving up on writing this book as doubts echoed in my mind, suggesting that I lacked the credibility to delve into the matter of "In His Kingdom." However, amidst this struggle, another voice emerged—one filled with encouragement. It reminded me that what truly matters is delivering the message regardless of how many copies are read. Even if the words within these pages touch one person, it will be a step forward in embracing God's kingdom.

With that encouragement resonating in my thoughts, I persevered. I poured myself into writing day and night, sacrificing meals and sleep because of my passion for sharing with you the divine artistry that shaped my life and ministry through God's hands. I hope that as you embark on this journey through the pages of "In His Kingdom ", you will find inspiration and encouragement—just as God's whispers sustained me throughout this writing process.

This book is a manifestation of my devotion to God, guided by the gentle whisper of the Holy Spirit. As I sat down to write, each word flowed through me with a force of inspiration from almighty God breaking free from the confines of traditional structure.

You'll encounter passages that stretch beyond brevity. They reach out like trees reaching for the heavens to capture the vast wisdom they aim to convey. Some may perceive these sections as lengthy or demanding. Hidden within their embrace lie profound revelations waiting to be discovered. Embrace them, my dear friend, for within their depths lies a wellspring of enlightenment.

In this book, there are instances where I have ventured beyond the boundaries set by writing rules. In the liberation of writing, I have discovered the essence of this book. It is my way of expressing my faith, a canvas where I have portrayed divine inspiration. While venturing off the beaten path to capture the ethereal, I aim to create a space for encounters with Godly wisdom.

Let this book be a reminder that even when the world appears to turn its back on us, the kingdom of God endures. It is a realm governed by love, compassion, and forgiveness, eagerly awaiting those who yearn to encounter its life-changing influence.

Together, let us venture forth on this path, placing our trust in God's guidance and illumination.

In His Kingdom,

Rosel Joy Bona

Dedication

I want to dedicate this to my wife, Irene, who has always been a supportive presence in my life. Your constant love, encouragement and faith in the God I believe in have been unwavering. When I look back on the journey we've shared, I am overwhelmed with gratitude for your support.

I apologize for the times I've missed out on moments with you and our family. Following God's calling has often taken me away from you more than I would have liked. Throughout it all, you're understanding and willingness to bear the weight of my absence have meant so much to me. Your selflessness and unwavering support have given me the drive to pursue my purpose with passion, knowing that you're always there waiting for me. Your love has been the driving force that propels me forward when faced with challenges. To our children, grandchildren and our Life Choice family, I will forever be grateful for the inspiration you provide. This dedication showcases our shared love, faith and unwavering commitment to the God who guides us.

I also want to dedicate this to all my children and grandchildren. Every one of you holds a place in my heart, and I am genuinely grateful to have you in my life. I understand that, at times, my decisions may not have aligned with your expectations, and for that, I apologize. I know that the path I chose for myself and our family may not have been what you envisioned. However, as I consistently reminded you, I firmly believed that my guidance would lead you towards a life of fulfilment and purpose.

If I have failed to meet your needs or live up to your expectations, please accept my apologies. I humbly ask for your forgiveness. I hope that one day, as each of you navigates your journeys in life, you will come to understand the choices made in service of our faith. Even though our paths may diverge, my heart remains filled with hope that each one of you will find your unique way of serving God. My love for all of you is unwavering, and should you seek it, I will always be here to offer guidance.

I dedicate this book to all the members of the Life Choice Church family; within its pages, I share the encouraging words derived from my experiences.

Every one of you has played a role in shaping my spiritual journey. Your steadfast faith, resilience and inner strength have constantly inspired me. I want to express my gratitude to all of you for being a true blessing in my life. It is because of your presence and unwavering support that I have been able to serve God with steadfast dedication.

I sincerely hope that this book stands as a testament to the love and faith that have guided us through our paths.

This book is dedicated to every soul who has been part of my journey. May it shine as a beacon of hope, inspiration and encouragement for you. May its words touch your hearts deeply, igniting a passion within you to fulfil your purpose and wholeheartedly serve God.

In His Kingdom,

Rosel Joy Bona

INTRODUCTION

In His Kingdom - Embarking on a Journey Through God's Life-Changing Kingdom presents an exploration that acts as a guide for our spiritual path. It delves into the teachings of Jesus Christ, allowing us to grasp and uncover insights about His kingdom.

Jesus consistently emphasized the significance of His kingdom, making it a central focus in His teachings than just briefly mentioning it. Through parables, He helped us understand the magnificence and humility, power and gentleness, justice and mercy embodied in the Kingdom of God.

This extraordinary book invites readers to delve into why Jesus considered the Kingdom of God so crucial in His teachings. Why did He encourage us to pray for its manifestation on Earth? What message did He intend for us to comprehend? What does it mean for each individual and humanity to seek His kingdom and experience it in our lives actively?

"In His Kingdom" goes beyond being a book; it serves as an invitation to embark on a journey. It is an expedition where we not only read Jesus' words but also live by them, where we don't simply intellectually understand His teachings but intensely experience their impact. It reminds us that His kingdom is not merely a promise for the future but can be realized here and now.

In every chapter, we will explore various aspects of God's Kingdom and uncover its profound impact on our lives. As you navigate through these pages, may your heart be touched, your faith and your understanding expanded. The wisdom you acquire along the way should inspire you to embrace the light and love of His Kingdom just as He did and serve others as He served. This journey isn't about learning about the Kingdom of God; it is an invitation to dwell within it, experience its essence, and actively engage in its unfolding.

Prepare yourself for an adventure that goes beyond knowledge—it offers transformation as well. By understanding why Jesus consistently emphasized the kingdom, we find a path toward a purpose-driven life. Let us embark on this voyage into the heart of God's Kingdom—a realm that possesses the power to transform lives.

Chapter One

In His Kingdom

---◆O◆---

Exploring the Call

The concept of God's Kingdom holds significance throughout both the Old and New Testaments. It is often referred to as the Kingdom of Heaven in the scriptures. During his time on Earth, Jesus frequently emphasized this concept through parables.

What does the term "Kingdom" truly represent? Simply put, it signifies God's reign manifested here on Earth—a realm where His authority extends not only over circumstances but also moulds hearts and minds. This divine dominion knows no boundaries; it exists as a profound truth wherever God's will be fulfilled.

Jesus often spoke about anticipating the arrival or realization of this glorious Kingdom. He taught us that God's Kingdom existed in the moment and future fulfilment. Throughout His ministry, He exemplified its presence through acts of healing, performing miracles, and preaching messages that brought salvation to all who listened.

However, He also discussed when He would return to establish His Kingdom.

To help people grasp the concept of the Kingdom of God and what it means to be a citizen within it, Jesus employed parables. One such legend speaks of a mustard seed, where Jesus compares the Kingdom of God and a seed that grows into a tree. This illustrates how the Kingdom may begin humbly but eventually expand and encompass every corner of the Earth.

In another called "The Wheat and Tares ", Jesus imparts that within the Kingdom, both forces of evil will exist at work. He warns that some individuals will attempt to infiltrate the kingdom and sow seeds of wickedness. However, in the end, goodness will triumph over evil.

Ultimately, the Kingdom of God symbolizes a realm characterized by peace, love and righteousness. It is where God's desires are realized fully, radiating His glory brightly.

As individuals who belong to His Kingdom, we are responsible for living in ways that reflect this reality. We must love God and treat our human beings with equal care and concern as we do for ourselves. We should prioritize seeking God's Kingdom and righteousness while understanding that everything else will fall into place.

The Bible contains references that shed light on why the Kingdom of God holds importance for believers like us.

Matthew 6:33 advises us to prioritize seeking His Kingdom above all else. By living in His sight, we can trust that all our needs will be cared for. This verse emphasizes the significance of making God's Kingdom our focus and relying on Him to provide for us.

When the Pharisees asked Jesus about when the Kingdom of God would come in Luke 17:20-21, Jesus responded by explaining that its arrival cannot be observed in a sense. It is not something localized but rather a reality within and among us.

In John 18:36, Jesus is recorded as saying that His Kingdom does not belong to this world. If it did, His followers would have fought to prevent His arrest by leaders. This verse teaches us that the Kingdom of God exists on a level beyond worldly realms and governments.

As believers, we must prioritize the Kingdom of God in our lives. Our goal should be to live in a way that reflects the values and principles upheld by His Kingdom. This includes living lives filled with love, justice and righteousness. It means managing the resources God gives us and using them to advance His Kingdom. Ultimately, it involves living in a manner that brings glory to God and shows others the reality of His Kingdom. We will explore how Jesus used stories called parables to explain the idea of the Kingdom of God and gain insights from them.

The Parable of the Sower (Matthew 13:1-23). This story illustrates the idea that the Kingdom of God can be compared to a seed planted in types of soil. Some people initially receive it with joy. Struggle when faced with challenges. Others accept the message of the Kingdom. Let worldly concerns and the allure of wealth overshadow it. Yet some embrace and nurture it, resulting in an outcome. The key lesson here is that accepting the Kingdom of God requires a heart and an effort to cultivate its teachings.

The Parable of the Mustard Seed (Matthew 13:31-32) teaches us that even though the Kingdom of God may start small, it will eventually grow and spread worldwide. Like a tiny mustard seed transforming into a tree, this Kingdom begins with only a few individuals. Still, it gradually becomes a powerful force impacting every corner of our planet.

The Parable of the Wheat and Tares (Matthew 13:24-30) emphasizes that good and evil will exist within the Kingdom of God. Similar to how wheat and weeds grow alongside each other in a field, true and false believers coexist in this realm. However, goodness will ultimately triumph over wickedness.

Lastly, we have the Parable of the Prodigal Son (Luke 15:11-32). This parable teaches us about the kindness and forgiveness found within the Kingdom of God. The father represents God, who warmly embraces and forgives his son despite his mistakes and failures. The underlying message is that no matter how far we may have strayed from our connection with God, He is always willing to welcome us with arms.

These examples provide a glimpse into the parables Jesus used to teach about the Kingdom of God. Each legend carries a lesson that helps us understand God's Kingdom and guides us to live by its values and principles.

The Enchanting Summons

As I sat in my study, a sensation washed over me. It felt like a divine force gently whispered into my soul, inviting me on a journey. I felt humbled and puzzled at that moment, questioning whether I deserved such an invitation.

"Who am I to accept or not accept such an offer?" I pondered, my mind filled with uncertainty and doubt. However, amidst my contemplation, a flicker of courage ignited within me. I recalled the teachings of scholars and authors whose words deeply resonated within my heart. Their wisdom provided solace and encouragement as their profound insights illuminated my path.

They discussed the impact of faith and its potential to foster personal growth and uncover the hidden greatness within each individual. It dawned on me that this invitation was not limited to me. Instead, it was open for anyone to dream and have faith.

Motivated by the timeless works of C.S. Lewis, I embarked on a journey of self-exploration and belief, eagerly immersing myself in the meaning behind this invitation. Through Lewis's words, I realized that Heaven's Kingdom is not confined to some realm but a state of being within oneself. It is a place where love, truth, and purpose intertwine harmoniously, casting light in life's darkest corners.

The teachings of Max Lucado taught me how to relinquish my doubts and fears to a power. In his book "For Nothing ", Lucado echoed the words of Jesus by encouraging us to entrust our burdens onto Him. Inspired by this wisdom, I emerged from the shadows of uncertainty. I wholeheartedly embraced this invitation with unwavering determination.

The writings of Priscilla Shirer served as my guiding compass on a quest towards self-discovery and gaining clarity about my life's purpose.

In her book named "Recognizing the Voice of God", she beautifully expresses a truth. Each of us is uniquely created with a purpose, and embracing this realization has given me the confidence to accept the invitation, knowing that I have the potential to make an impact on the world around me.

Moved by the teachings of these authors and biblical scholars, I embarked on a journey of self-reflection and spiritual growth. Through prayer, meditation and diligent study of scriptures, I began to unravel the mysteries surrounding my existence. In this process, I discovered that the invitation extended to me was not burdensome but rather an opportunity to embrace life fully.

As I pen down these words, my heart is filled with wonder and gratitude. The intimidating and overwhelming invitation has become a source of inspiration and purpose. It reminds me of 2 Timothy 1:7, which says, "For God has not given us a spirit of fear but one of power, love and self-discipline." With this assurance in mind, I take a breath and step boldly into the awe-inspiring unknown that awaits me.

The Invitation to Release and Walk with Him.

In the realm of destiny, the longing to let go and journey alongside God surpasses any words and becomes irresistible. It is a beckoning that compels us to step out of our comfort zones and embrace a life imbued with purpose and significance. The story of my path commences deep within my soul, where my heart yielded to the gentle whisper of divine love, grace and transformation.

Reflecting upon the encounters and invaluable lessons I've acquired, I am reminded of the profound words articulated by biblical scholars. John Piper eloquently captures the essence of this calling in his book "Don't Waste Your Life," which beautifully expresses that "God shines radiantly through us when we find our utmost fulfilment in Him." This profound truth serves as a reminder that genuine contentment lies not in pursuing desires but in wholeheartedly dedicating ourselves to the One who masterfully orchestrates every step we take.

Recalling Jesus' teachings, we are prompted to remember His invitation to surrender and follow Him. He said, "If anyone desires to come after me, let them renounce themselves daily, take up their cross and walk in my footsteps" (Luke 9:23 ESV).

These words remind us that true discipleship requires letting go of our desires and ambitions. John MacArthur, a known biblical scholar, explores this idea further in his book "The Gospel According to Jesus." He emphasizes the importance of answering Christ's call by surrendering ourselves and accepting His authority. MacArthur explains that surrendering to Christ means giving Him control over our lives and acknowledging Him as our ultimate Lord and Master (MacArthur, 2008, p. 32).

This newfound understanding allowed me to personalize my connection with Him, embracing my strengths and preferences as I sought His presence.

In moments of uncertainty and scepticism, the Bible became a haven for me, a wellspring of wisdom that guided me toward surrender. The words of the Apostle Paul in his letter to the Romans resonated within me, reminding me of the incredible power of faith." conforming to the world's influence renews your mind for authentic transformation." This verse guided my thoughts, actions, and choices toward a life steeped in obedience and fulfilment.

May you discover the bravery to release your fears and embrace the love bestowed upon you by the One who intricately designed your purpose.

May your spirit be awakened by the Divine Invitation as it ignites your faith and empowers you to embrace the call to surrender and follow Him. Through this, you will experience a transformation that impacts your own life but also touches the lives of countless others. Let's embark on this journey together, fully aware of the incredible blessings that await us on this less-travelled path.

Throughout my upbringing, I often felt a sense of inadequacy. The world seemed vast and overwhelming, and I constantly compared myself to others who appeared to have everything figured out. Feelings of unworthiness consumed me, making me wonder if I would ever truly grasp the essence of a calling.

In moments of despair, I sought solace in the wisdom shared by scholars and authors who had walked similar paths. Their words became a guiding light in my life, leading me to gain an understanding of God's calling to His Kingdom. Through their teachings, I learned to embrace the idea that my *"limitations do not define me. Instead, it presents an opportunity for God's grace and purpose to shine through."*

The scriptures provided comfort and inspiration as I immersed myself in their pages. The stories of Moses, David and even the apostle Paul echoed a message: God often chooses individuals who may seem unlikely to fulfil His intentions. Even they had doubts about their worthiness. Their lives served as evidence of the power of embracing God's calls.

As I delved deeper into the scriptures, I realized that God's invitation to His Kingdom is not limited to a select few; it is extended to anyone willing to respond to His call. The notion of being unworthy began unravelling as I understood that God's grace washes away our inadequacies and declares us worthy through the sacrifice of Jesus Christ, His Son.

This newfound understanding breathed life into my journey. I ignited a fire within me to embrace God's call with determination courageously. I learned that comprehending His Kingdom is not about our abilities or achievements but surrendering ourselves to His guidance.

During moments of uncertainty and doubt, I often seek solace in the words of C.S. Lewis, a Christian author who emphasized that God does not expect perfection from us but desires our willingness to follow Him. This powerful truth comforts me, reminding me that God's calling goes beyond our limitations and guides us towards a purpose that surpasses our comprehension. I want to share the challenges and victories I encountered while exploring the concept of God's calling and embracing its impact. My goal is to provide you with encouragement and inspiration, reminding you that you deserve to respond to His call on any doubts or feelings of inadequacy.

As we embark on this journey together, let us find the strength to set aside our uncertainties and insecurities, opening ourselves up to the opportunity of being part of His Kingdom. Let us remember that our worthiness lies solely in His grace.

In fact, our sense of inadequacy or unworthiness becomes a testament to the grace and mercy of God as He works through imperfect vessels.

While researching, I stumbled upon a book by John Hamilton, a biblical scholar, titled "Embracing the Divine Call." His teachings deeply captivated me as he eloquently explained that God's call doesn't hinge on our abilities or achievements but stems from His love for us. Hamilton emphasized that human standards cannot confine the vastness of God's Kingdom; it transcends all limitations.

Furthermore, Hamilton delved into the concept that feeling inadequate or unworthy is precisely what qualifies us for entry into God's Kingdom. In our humility, we recognize our need for a Saviour and can wholeheartedly embrace His call. In our weakness, His strength shines through perfectly—a sentiment beautifully expressed by the apostle Paul in 2 Corinthians 12:9.

This newfound understanding pushed me forward, giving me the courage to continue my journey. I immersed myself in the writings of scholars like Sarah Young, who authored the deeply moving devotional "Jesus Calling." Her genuine vulnerability and unwavering trust in God's goodness inspired me to let go of my doubts and fears. Through her writings, I discovered that answering God's call requires taking a leap of faith and surrendering my weaknesses and insecurities daily to the loving God who invites me.

Motivated by these teachings, I began incorporating them into my life, finding solace and purpose in embracing God's Kingdom. I embarked on a relationship with Him, understanding that embracing His call is a journey. It is not a destination but a transformative process that continues to shape and mould me.

Reflecting on my experiences and the wisdom gained from scholars and authors, I am compelled to share this message of hope and encouragement. This book serves as an invitation for all those who have felt a stirring in their hearts—a calling that draws them towards something. I encourage you to explore the references mentioned and delve into the writings of these scholars and authors. Allow their words to resonate within your heart deeply. May this journey towards embracing His purpose bring you closer to a profound comprehension of God's Kingdom and your unique place.

A Journey of Self-Reflection: Embracing Our Calling

When we are called to join His Kingdom, even if we feel inadequate or unworthy, it becomes a journey that requires deep introspection, faith and seeking guidance. This paragraph acts as a stone in this journey by guiding us in acknowledging and navigating our feelings of inadequacy and unworthiness.

When we receive a calling, we often face a sense of inadequacy or feel unworthy. These emotions can stem from our perceived limitations, past failures, or simply being aware of our human weaknesses. However, we must recognize and accept these feelings as part of the process.

As we embark on this journey, there is solace and encouragement in the psalmist's words. Psalm 139:14 (NIV) says, *"I praise you because I am fearfully and wonderfully made; your works are wonderful; I know that well."* This verse serves as a reminder that despite feeling inadequate at times, God Himself has fearfully and wonderfully created each of us. Embracing this truth allows us to shift our focus from dwelling on our perceived shortcomings to recognizing the potential within each individual.

Priscilla Shirer, an author and speaker, sheds light on the importance of seeking guidance in comprehending and embracing the call in her book "Discerning the Voice of God." Shirer encourages us to rely on God's wisdom and advice when we feel inadequate. She points out that it is during our moments of unworthiness or inadequacy that God's strength shines through (Shirer, 2012, p. 89). Shirer's words remind us that our perceived weaknesses can become opportunities for God to demonstrate His power and strength through us.

A plea to seek guidance and assistance

When it comes to answering God's call and embracing His Kingdom, it is vital to recognize the significance of seeking guidance and support. Along our path towards accepting this calling, reaching out to a mentor, pastor, or a trusted individual can play an essential role. They can offer advice and support as we navigate our emotions and discern the path before us.

Responding to a call can be overwhelming as doubts and uncertainties arise. That is why seeking guidance from someone who has walked a path or possesses spiritual wisdom becomes invaluable. They can provide insights that help us explore our emotions, clarify our thoughts, and accompany us as we embark on this journey.

In his book "The Purpose Driven Life ", esteemed Christian author Rick Warren emphasizes the significance of seeking guidance and support in comprehending and embracing our unique calling. He reminds us that God never intended for us to go through life; instead, He desires to be with us every step of the way (Warren, 2002, p. 87). These words from Warren remind us that we shouldn't attempt to navigate this journey in isolation but should rely on the wisdom and support of others.

Moreover, in his letter to the Ephesians, the Apostle Paul encourages believers to seek guidance and support from leaders. He emphasizes that God has appointed apostles, prophets, evangelists, pastors and teachers to equip and empower the saints for their ministry tasks (Ephesians 4:11-12 NKJV). This passage from the Bible highlights the role played by spiritual mentors and pastors in assisting and guiding believers as they pursue their divine calling.

Understanding and embracing the concept of being summoned into His Kingdom is a step in this journey. One crucial aspect of this process involves delving into your faith through in-depth study. This paragraph emphasizes the importance of immersing yourself in texts, teachings and theological resources that delve into the concept of a divine calling. By engaging with these writings, we can understand the journeys undertaken by prophets, disciples and other spiritual figures who have answered their holy calling.

This section encourages us to strengthen our faith by engaging with texts, teachings and theological resources. Through these explorations, we can gain insight into the journeys of those who have embraced their callings and realize that feelings of inadequacy are common and surmountable.

A Call to Embrace Self-Compassion

When understanding and embracing the idea of being called to God's Kingdom, being kind and gentle towards oneself is crucial. Throughout this journey, practising self-compassion becomes essential. Remember that experiencing feelings of inadequacy or unworthiness is something many individuals face at some point in their lives. It should not define your value or worthiness. Cultivating self-compassion involves acknowledging your strengths, accepting your flaws, and treating yourself with love and understanding.

When you embark on a journey to answer a calling, facing moments of self-doubt and inadequacy is natural. However, it's important to remember that these emotions do not diminish your worth or potential. Revered figures in religious texts like Moses, David or Peter experienced uncertainty and insecurity.

By recognizing that these feelings are part of our shared humanity, you can begin to cultivate self-compassion and show kindness towards yourself.

Practicing self-compassion entails embracing your strengths while also accepting your imperfections. Acknowledge the gifts and talents you possess. Celebrate them as an essential aspect of your divine purpose. At the time, I understand that nobody is perfect, as imperfections are inherent in being human. Recognize that these imperfections can serve as opportunities for growth and learning. Realize they maintain your value and ability to respond to a calling.

Showing yourself love and compassion is a part of practising self-care. Be gentle with yourself when facing challenges or setbacks along the way. Offer words of encouragement to yourself. Remind yourself that you are inherently deserving of love and respect. Always remember that God's love and grace are there to guide and support you on your journey.

A call to connect with a community

When embracing the concept of being called to His Kingdom, another crucial aspect is considering the power of connecting with like-minded individuals who also explore their divine callings. This connection can bring benefits. Exchanging stories, uncertainties and achievements, you can gain insights and find inspiration, reminding yourself that you're not alone in your journey.

Pursuing a calling, it becomes essential to surround yourself with a community. This community might consist of believers, mentors or individuals who have already ventured down a path. By connecting with others who are also exploring their callings, you'll discover a sense of belonging and camaraderie.

Engaging with a community opens opportunities to share experiences and learn from one another. Through conversations about your journey, you can uncover fresh perspectives and insights that may not have occurred to you otherwise. Hearing about the challenges others face and their triumphs can provide encouragement and motivation as you navigate your calling. It's important to acknowledge that obstacles exist, but growth and fulfilment are also parts of this journey.

Apart from sharing experiences, being part of a community grants an avenue for expressing doubts and uncertainties well. It's perfectly normal to have questions or moments of tension along the way. One way to find reassurance and guidance is by discussing these doubts with others who are treading a path. Often, some individuals have experienced doubts and can offer valuable insights or perspectives to help you navigate them.

In the book titled "The Purpose Driven Life: What on Earth Am I For?" by Rick Warren, valuable insights are shared regarding the significance of being part of a community and embracing one's purpose. Warren emphasizes that we are designed to thrive in a community to foster fellowship and to be a part of a family unit. According to him, none of us can genuinely fulfil the purposes intended by God (Warren, 2002, p. 124).

As you explore and accept your calling within His Kingdom, it is vital to recognize the importance of connecting with a community. Engage with minded individuals who are also seeking divine callings because you can find inspiration and guidance by sharing experiences, doubts and victories. Becoming part of a community will give you support, advice, and a sense of belonging throughout your journey.

A beckoning towards prayer and contemplation

Embracing the concept of being summoned by God into His Kingdom has another consideration. Engaging in prayer, They are engaging in invitation practices. These activities enable you to connect with a higher power while finding inner tranquillity within yourself. Through prayer and meditation comes clarity that assists in overcoming feelings of inadequacy by gathering the strength for personal growth.

Prayer is a tool for communicating with God and seeking His guidance and support. It allows you to express your desires, concerns and gratitude, fostering a connection with the divine. During moments of prayer, you can find solace, comfort and reassurance in knowing you are not alone on your journey.

Meditation involves quieting the mind and focusing on the moment. Practising mindfulness and embracing stillness creates space for wisdom to enter your life. Through meditation, you can let go of distractions and negative thoughts, enabling you to tap into yourself and establish a connection with the divine presence within.

Both prayer and meditation provide opportunities for self-reflection and introspection. They allow you to delve into your thoughts, emotions and aspirations to gain clarity and understanding about your purpose. By following these practices, you can discover the path that aligns with your true calling while receiving guidance on navigating it.

In embracing the concept of being called to His Kingdom, always remember the importance of prayer and meditation. Engaging in these practices allows you to establish a connection, tap into peace, find clarity, and gather the strength needed to overcome feelings of inadequacy.

A Journey Embracing the Divine Call

When understanding and embracing the concept of a divine call to His Kingdom, it's essential to recognize that this doesn't happen overnight. It's a journey that spans a lifetime, requiring growth and transformation. To embark on this journey, taking steps to embrace the call is advisable.

Taking steps allows you to adapt slowly to the changes and challenges accompanying a divine calling. This process helps build confidence and reaffirms your connection with the purpose. One effective way to begin is by engaging in acts of service and volunteering. By offering your time and skills to help others, you align yourself with love, compassion and selflessness—values at the core of any call.

Deepening your practices plays a crucial role in embracing this divine calling. This may involve dedicating time for prayer, meditation, studying scriptures or participating in religious gatherings. These practices lay a foundation for spiritual growth while fostering a profound connection with the divine.

In his book "The Purpose Driven Life ", Rick Warren shares insights on how to take those small steps to embrace their divine calling. Warren emphasizes the significance of starting with achievable actions that align with our purpose. He famously says, "The journey of a thousand miles begins with one step" (Warren, 2002, p. 34). By taking these steps, we can gradually align our lives with the divine calling and make a meaningful impact in His Kingdom.

We don't have to give up everything. Instead, we gain what truly matters.

Throughout life's journey, we often search for something beyond our existence. Something that brings meaning, fulfilment and enduring significance. In our quest for God's Kingdom, we understand the truth. We don't sacrifice everything; instead, we acquire what holds genuine value. Through this pursuit, the layers that obscure our true essence unravel and reveal our purpose and identity in Him.

As we journey towards God's Kingdom, it becomes evident that our earthly pursuits often distract us from discovering our identity. Myles Munroe highlights that our true identity is not based on achievements, possessions or societal status. Instead, it is found in our connection with the Creator Himself. He reminds us that even before we were formed in our mother's womb, God knew us intimately and designed each of us with a purpose within His Kingdom (Munroe, 2002).

Therefore, seeking God's Kingdom brings us closer to Him and allows us to rediscover our authentic selves crafted meticulously by divine power.

Throughout our journey towards His Kingdom, we often encounter trials and challenges. However, these difficulties serve as opportunities for growth and strengthening our faith. In his book "The Purpose Driven Life ", Rick Warren reminds us that God works in ways and orchestrates every circumstance for our ultimate benefit. He emphasizes the importance of understanding that we were created by God and for God to find meaning in life (Warren, 2002). When we have faith in His guidance, we realize that during times of hardship, we are being shaped into vessels that reflect His glory and fulfil the purpose of His Kingdom.

As we gradually immerse ourselves in pursuing God's Kingdom, we gain insight into the nature of worldly possessions. Theologian A.W. Tozer once said that anything that hinders our connection with God becomes an adversary regardless of society's acceptance or usefulness (Tozer, 1986). This means that the world's treasures can never compare to the abundance found within God's Kingdom.

As we journey through life, we come to understand the importance of having a perspective. We realize that our actions and efforts hold weight and have lasting effects beyond the present moment.

You were intricately designed to be extraordinary.

In the expanse of the universe, among countless stars scattered across the dark sky, lies a profound meaning ingrained within each of us.

We weren't just made to be people but intricately crafted to possess extraordinary qualities within God's Kingdom. This incredible potential lies dormant within our souls, patiently awaiting its awakening and embrace.

Esteemed scholars and Christian writers have diligently explored this truth throughout the Bible like a symphony of wisdom echoing through time. One of these scholars is John Piper, who beautifully elaborates on our purpose and calling in his book "Desiring God." He reminds us that our human limitations don't confine or restrict God's plan for us. In fact, His vision for our lives exceeds our comprehension and imagination. As skilled sculptors meticulously mould every aspect of their masterpieces with purpose and intention, God shapes us into royalty in His Kingdom.

As believers, we find solace and inspiration in the words penned by Christian author Max Lucado. In his book "You'll Get Through This ", Lucado reassures us that we are never alone on our journey. Our lives are embraced by God's grace—a wellspring of love and mercy that knows no bounds. Despite our flaws and shortcomings, we take comfort in the encompassing grace of God regardless of how far we may have strayed. Through this grace, we unlock the incredible potential that resides within us.

In God's Kingdom, perfection is not the standard; He values our faithfulness as His children. In her book "Unashamed" Christian author Christine Caine sheds light on this truth. She encourages us to embrace our qualities, step out boldly in faith, and trust God's provisions. Caine reminds us that our worth and value are not tied to achievements or recognition but are rooted in following God's calling.

As we reflect on the wisdom these scholars and Christian writers shared, we are reminded of the extraordinary destiny that awaits us. We are called to rise above mediocrity and fully embrace the purpose intricately woven into us by God. Our potential knows no limits as it surpasses failures or insecurities; it thrives when we surrender ourselves to His plan.

My friends let us stand with unwavering confidence, knowing we were uniquely designed to embody greatness within God's Kingdom. May we embrace a renewed sense of direction enveloped in the grace bestowed upon us and encouraged by unwavering faith. As we journey through life's path, let our lives bear witness to the love and strength emanating from our Divine Creator. In the scheme of things, we must prioritize developing a meaningful connection with the divine.

Amidst the busyness and chaos of our lives, we must remember that God's Kingdom always has time for us. Let us ensure that we stay aware of our routines to acknowledge His presence. Our utmost focus should be on nurturing a significant bond with the divine.

Time flows ceaselessly, unaffected by the hustle and bustle of our existence. Within this realm, His Kingdom resides, patiently awaiting our arrival. In this clockwork, every movement aligns perfectly with His divine purpose. He never becomes too preoccupied to extend His grace and love to those seeking Him earnestly.

As we journey through life, we often find ourselves consumed by demands and distractions surrounding us. Our schedules overflow with appointments, obligations and ending tasks. It's too easy to get caught up in this whirlwind of busyness and lose sight of what matters.

According to Charles Stanley, a pastor and writer, "our primary focus should always be our connection with God. It should be the foundation upon which everything else is built." These words offer wisdom that encourages us to re-evaluate our priorities and align them with God's timing. By making God the centre of our existence, we can genuinely experience His love. Find peace amidst life's chaos.

A scholar, Matthew Henry, beautifully expresses this truth by stating that "someone too busy to pray is more active than what God intended them to be." This thought-provoking statement touches our hearts. It prompts us to reconsider how we manage our time. It encourages us to pause, reflect and redirect our attention towards nurturing a connection with the divine.

As we embark on this journey of faith, let us turn to the words of Henry Blackaby—an author within the Christian community. Blackaby urges us to "seek God's will and align our lives accordingly." He emphasizes that our connection with the divine adds to our existence and the foundation for our lives.

Our lives are deeply intertwined with God's timetable, where His Kingdom eagerly awaits our presence. Amidst all the chaos and busyness, it is vital to avoid becoming too absorbed to spend quality time with Him. Our utmost priority should be nurturing a relationship with the divine.

Your unwavering faith, like ocean waves, stands as an enduring testament.

Throughout history's depths, where persecution and adversity threaten to suppress the faithful, a tale is whispered from one generation to another. It serves as a reminder that despite trials, the Kingdom of God persists with unwavering resilience and steadfast faith.

As we explore the depths of history, we find inspiration in those individuals who clung steadfastly to their beliefs despite the dangers they faced. From the Christians who bravely confronted lions in arenas to the brave heroes of the Reformation who fearlessly stood against the oppressive forces of their time, their stories echo through the corridors of time and continue to resonate with us today.

An exceptional illustration of unwavering faith can be found in the tale of Job. Job firmly believed in God's power and goodness amid tragedy and suffering. After losing his wealth, family and health, Job proclaimed with unwavering conviction, "Even if He takes my life, I will still have hope in Him" (Job 13:15). His resolute faith exemplified the strength that resides within the spirit when it is anchored upon God's steadfast promises.

The strength of faith is not limited to the heroes we encounter within biblical narratives; it reverberates throughout history in the lives of believers. One such example can be witnessed in Corrie Ten Boom's story—a woman from the Netherlands—who, along with her family, risked everything to protect Jews during the Holocaust. Despite enduring cruelty while imprisoned in a Nazi concentration camp Corrie clung to her trust in God. She once said, "There is no depth of despair that God's love cannot reach." Her unwavering faith in God's power and unconditional love brought hope to those who suffered alongside her.

Their steadfast belief challenges us to confront our trials with courage, reminding us that in the fiercest storms, His Kingdom remains unshakable.

So wide, so deep, and filled with wonders yet to be discovered.

As I strolled along the Cronulla Esplanade holding my granddaughter in my arms, the tranquil rhythm of the sea caught my attention. The waves crashing against the shore mirrored how my heart swelled whenever I glanced at the slumbering beauty resting in my embrace.

At that moment, a whisper resonated within me, unmistakably conveying the voice of a presence. *"The kingdom of God is like this sea,"* He said, *"so wide, so deep, and filled with wonders yet to be discovered. Your mission is to share the message of my Kingdom with others while I take care of everything."*

Tears filled my eyes as I absorbed the truth behind those words. It felt like floodgates had burst inside me, flooding me with inspiration that needed to be captured before it slipped away. With a sense of purpose, I gently settled my granddaughter into her stroller. I returned home to my writing desk, determined to document these thoughts and revelations racing through my mind.

Sitting at my desk surrounded by shelves filled with books and journals brimming with biblical insights, I couldn't help but feel a deep reverence. I was fortunate to have access to the wisdom of biblical scholars. A devoted Christian writers who had dedicated their lives to unravelling the intricate tapestry of God's teachings. Their words became pillars that supported the inspiration flowing from within me.

I delved into the reservoir of biblical references with every stroke of the keyboard, conscientiously attributing sources and crafting a comprehensive bibliography. The pages of this book gradually filled with tales, parables and lessons taught by Jesus himself, intricately woven with my personal experiences and reflections. It became a fusion of ancient wisdom and profound revelations—a testament to the magnificence of God's divine guidance.

Throughout this journey, moments of doubt occasionally tried to infiltrate my thoughts. What if no one reads my book? What if my book goes unnoticed? Like a soft breeze on a calm day, the gentle voice of the Lord would whisper encouragement into my ears—a constant reminder that *"success should not be measured by worldly standards alone but rather by being an instrument in delivering God's message and spreading His Kingdom."*

Days turned into weeks, which soon transformed into months as I wholeheartedly dedicated myself to this inspiring endeavour.

The support and guidance I received from fellow believers in Christ were precious. We aimed to empower and uplift each other, reminding ourselves that our efforts had an impact, even if they touched just one person's soul.

Finally, the day arrived when I finished writing my book. Holding the manuscript in my hands, I felt overwhelming gratitude for the journey that led me here. It wasn't merely a book; it stood as a testament to the presence that filled my heart while strolling alongside my granddaughter on the heavenly shores.

With trembling hands, I distributed copies to biblical scholars and Christian authors whose works influenced and shaped my writing. Their responses filled me with joy as they commended the depth of insight and clarity in my writing. A profound sense of wonder engulfed me as I realized I had become a vessel through which God's message reached others.

The path could have been smoother. It was undeniably glorious and rewarding. The inspiration that coursed through me on that day at Esplanade had now touched lives through the pages of my book.

So, whenever you find yourself uncertain, my dear friends, think about the ocean's vastness and how many marvellous things are still waiting to be discovered. Have faith in the inspiration that fills your heart as it comes from a source. Embrace your role as a messenger of God's Kingdom with devotion and trust that

He will care for everything. May you experience the exhilaration and happiness of fulfilling your purpose and spreading His love worldwide.

When we align our hopes and ambitions with the Kingdom of God, something extraordinary happens—they shine brighter than the stars. The key is prioritizing seeking His Kingdom above all else and watching our dreams flourish on His canvas.

As we prioritize God's Kingdom above everything, it's natural for uncertainties to arise; however, during those times when our faith wavers, we find comfort in the assurance that God will take care of everything we need.

These profound words spoken by our Creator hold timeless truth. Serve as a guiding light even in the darkest moments. When we make seeking God's Kingdom our priority and trust in Him while aligning our desires with His will, we can be confident that not only will our needs be met, but they will also be exceeded.

Biblical scholars have delved deeply into this promise, highlighting its significance and practical application. One such scholar is N.T. Wright emphasizes the Kingdom of God as Jesus' central focus and encourages us to prioritize it. In his book "Surprised by Hope ", Wright reminds us that when we wholeheartedly seek God's Kingdom and align ourselves with His purpose, we can have unwavering confidence in His provision and faithfulness.

Christian authors have also expressed their perspectives on this transformative promise, inspiring us to have faith in the goodness and sovereignty of our Heavenly Father. In his book "Trusting God: When Life Hurts ", Jerry Bridges reminds us that "trusting God's promises requires a trust beyond human understanding." Bridges suggests that by placing our faith in His love, our doubts fade away, and we find comfort in knowing He will abundantly provide everything we truly need.

Throughout texts, we encounter numerous instances where God's faithfulness is evident through His provision for His children. Whether it be the manna provided during the journey, through the wilderness or the multiplication of loaves and fishes, these examples consistently remind us that when we prioritize seeking His Kingdom, our needs will be met beyond what we can comprehend.

This promise is genuinely captivating and inspiring! It fills our hearts with hope, courage and unwavering trust, urging us to prioritize treasures over illusions. When we focus on the eternal and align our lives with God's plan, we discover a joy and contentment that surpasses the pleasures of this world.

May we be captivated by the invitation to trust wholeheartedly, letting go of any lingering doubts as we embrace the power of making God's reign a priority in our lives. Through this surrender, we find peace, abundant provision and fulfilment for our desires.

The blending of all the instruments created a symphony that resonated with perfect harmony.

One morning, as the sun began to rise and painted the sky with hues of pink and orange, I found myself settling into my spot for my morning moments of reflection. With a heart seeking guidance and inspiration, I opened my Bible. I started reading. Later, I began to realize that within those pages lay a tale that would unfold before me, leading me to a profound moment of realization and connection with God.

Lost in my devotions, a gentle melody softly played in the background. Intrigued by its captivating tune, I paused to immerse myself in the music, not wanting to miss even a single note. It was a worship song called "Lilim" (Shelter) by Victory Worship Philippines, sung in the Tagalog language. From the first moment, its harmonious melodies reached my ears, I sensed that something extraordinary was about to transpire.

The song wrapped around me like an embrace, a soothing balm for my soul. He filled me with wonderment. The lyrics of this song deeply resonated with me, serving as a reminder of God's love and faithfulness. With each verse and chorus, it felt as if His presence drew closer as if He used this music to touch the essence of my being.

However, what truly captivated me was not the lyrics themselves. How all the instruments seamlessly blended to create a symphony that emanated harmony. The piano flowed like rain, the guitars were strummed with precision and tenderness, and the drums provided a steady heartbeat. It felt as though they were weaving a masterpiece of artistry.

As I closed my eyes and surrendered myself to God's embrace, I heard a whisper in the depths of my soul. It was a voice filled with wisdom. Laced with humour and said, *"You see,"* it gently spoke, *"This is quite similar to my Kingdom. I am the conductor, and every symphony must play their designated notes."*

That moment became an epiphany for me—a glimpse into the purpose and beauty found in the diversity within the body of Christ. Just as each instrument has its role in creating a symphony, every individual has a unique part to play in this magnificent orchestration we call life. No position is insignificant because every person's contribution adds to God's awe-inspiring composition.

That revelation gave me a deep appreciation for my purpose in God's Kingdom. Whether I take the stage with a leading melody or offer support, I realize that each note I play can bring glory to Him.

I am unique, intricately crafted, and perfectly positioned to fulfil a purpose specifically designed for me.

This realization became a guiding light as I entered the world that day. Inspired by the lyrics of "Lilim" and its shared wisdom, I intended to embrace my calling and live a life honouring God in all aspects. Understanding my place within God's Kingdom compelled me to inspire others to uncover their purpose and wholeheartedly embrace it.

As the song lyrics of "Lilim" touch the body of Christ as it has touched me. May the heavenly whisper I encountered that morning serve as a source of inspiration for you, too. Like a symphony comes alive through harmonizing every instrument, each person has an important role. Embrace your gifts, talents and calling confidently, knowing that God—the conductor—will lovingly guide you to perform your part excellently.

In this symphony called life, each individual is assigned a particular role, much like in an orchestra, where every instrument serves a specific purpose. It's crucial to remember that our responsibility is not to oversee the ensemble but rather to focus on playing our devices to the best of our abilities (Piper, 2010). This understanding profoundly resonates with the wisdom expressed in texts.

John Piper, a scholar of the Bible and a Christian writer, beautifully illustrates the connection between humanity and God. He explains that just as a composer and conductor leads an orchestra, God serves as the composer and conductor while we serve as His instruments. This concept reinforces the belief that our lives have a purpose and are part of a planned arrangement (Piper, 2010).

Furthermore, in the book of Jeremiah, this timeless truth is highlighted through a proclamation that emphasizes God's awareness of His plans for us. The verse states, "For I am aware of the plans I have for you ", declares the Lord. "Plans to prosper you and not to harm you; plans to give you hope and a promising future" (Jeremiah 29:11). This verse fills us with hope and reassurance by affirming that the conductor of our lives has prepared a symphony specifically tailored for each one of us. However, it's important to mention that playing our instrument to the best of our abilities requires discipline, dedication and perseverance (Foster, 1998). Like musicians who diligently practice refining their skills, we must nurture our gifts and talents with God's guidance.

Furthermore, remember that we follow God as our conductor who orchestrates everything from His Kingdom above. As C.S. Lewis eloquently expresses, "God pays attention to each of us." We connect with God as if we were the only beings He ever created. This reminds us of the importance of seeking God's presence and guidance.

Amid life's chaos and busyness, losing sight of our purpose is easy. However, the book of Psalms offers comfort and inspiration by advising us to acknowledge and trust that God is in control (Psalm 46:10). This verse encourages us to rely on Him for clarity and direction.

Ultimately, we truly desire our unique qualities to blend harmoniously like a symphony. We can achieve this by embracing God's guidance and showing love towards Him and others (Keller, 2016).

Our role in the symphony of life isn't about leading but playing our parts to the best of our abilities. It's crucial to remember that God, who orchestrates from His Kingdom, has a beautiful symphony planned for each of us. Drawing inspiration from scholars and Christian writers, we should nurture our talents through disciplined practice, find comfort in God's presence, and wholeheartedly submit ourselves to Him.

A shining light and steadfast presence in the unpredictable waves of life.

The metaphor of the Kingdom of God being likened to a lighthouse holds power and profoundly resonates with those seeking guidance and hope. Like a lighthouse provides sailors safety, direction and resilience during storms, the Kingdom of God is a shining light and steadfast presence in the unpredictable waves of life.

To truly grasp the symbolism behind comparing the Kingdom of God to a lighthouse, it is essential to understand the essence of lighthouses themselves. Lighthouses go beyond being structures; they embody safety, guidance and strength in times of adversity. Their beams pierce through the darkness, warning sailors about the waters and guiding them away from dangerous rocks. Similarly, the Kingdom of God is an illuminating force amidst life's uncertainties—offering solace, empowerment and unwavering optimism.

The Bible contains passages that hint at the role played by the Kingdom of God as a lighthouse. Isaiah 60:1 proclaims with conviction, "Arise! Shine! Your light has arrived; the glory of Yahweh is shining upon you. In this context, the light represents more than knowledge or understanding; it symbolizes God's divine presence that guides and illuminates our paths. We find clarity and hope in life's most challenging trials within this realm.

The Apostle Paul reinforces this imagery in his letter to the Ephesians. He writes, "You were once surrounded by darkness, but now you are enlightened in the Lord. Live your lives as children of light" (Ephesians 5:8). Paul reminds us that through our faith, we become bearers of this light. Our responsibility is to shine brightly in a world overshadowed by darkness and offer glimpses of God's Kingdom to those lost and searching.

Throughout history, Christian writers and scholars have delved into the concept of God's Kingdom as a beacon that provides insights deepening our understanding of this truth. C.S. Lewis ponders the significance of faith as a guiding light in his book Mere Christianity. He expresses, "God assumed form to transform creatures into sons and daughters—not merely refining individuals into versions of themselves but creating an entirely new kind of being. It is akin to turning a horse into a winged creature than just teaching it to jump higher. "Lewis beautifully captures the impact of the Kingdom of God, which guides our steps and shapes us into individuals capable of triumphing over life's challenges.

In times of uncertainty, the Kingdom of God remains a beacon of hope. As we navigate life's trials, we are reminded that we are never alone. John Piper eloquently said, "God is most glorified in us when we find our satisfaction in Him." The Kingdom invites us to discover contentment, hope and purpose in Him. It encourages us to focus on the light that never fades and assures us that it will lead us home. Let's find solace in the psalmist's words, who proclaimed, "Your word is a guiding light for my journey" (Psalm 119:105). May this divine illumination brighten our lives, ignite our spirits, and inspire us to share hope with those still in the haze of uncertainty.

Let it be your passion rather than an obligation to prioritize His Kingdom as your utmost priority. Shift your mindset from a sense of duty to one filled with gratitude for this opportunity and witness the transformative power it will unfold within your life.

As believers, we understand the importance of placing God at the centre of our lives. However, moving beyond duty and embracing a genuine passion for His Kingdom is crucial. When we shift our mindset from feeling obligated to considering it a privilege to prioritize God, we unlock transformations through His limitless love.

The Gospel of Matthew reminds us of the significance of seeking God's Kingdom above everything. Matthew 6:33 (NIV) emphasizes that all other necessary things will be provided by seeking His Kingdom and living righteously. This verse highlights the value and underscores the necessity for placing God's Kingdom at the forefront. Esteemed Bible scholar D.A. Carson further delves into this passage, underscoring that believers should pursue "integrity of heart and obedience to God's will" (Carson, 2010, p. 1306). Therefore, seeking God's blessings and aligning our hearts and desires with His righteous plan is crucial.

When we transform our perspective from seeing our commitment as an obligation to recognizing it as a privilege, we experience a paradigm shift. It can be tempting to view serving in God's Kingdom as burdensome or obligatory. However, as we grasp the privilege of being God's children and representatives, our hearts overflow with enthusiasm and gratitude.

In his book titled "Where the Bible Speaks to You "Christian writer W.A. Criswell beautifully captures this sentiment; "Serving the living God is a privilege—an occurrence for you or anyone—to serve His kingdom and righteousness" (Criswell, 1993 p. 245). Embracing an attitude of willingness rather than obligation allows us to discover joy in actively participating in God's redemptive work here on Earth.

Choosing the passion of feeling obligated requires nurturing a personal relationship with God. By spending time in His presence through prayer and studying His Word, our hearts naturally ignite with enthusiasm for His Kingdom. In his book "Mere Christianity" esteemed Christian author C.S. Lewis eloquently describes this experience; "The moment we realize that this passion doesn't come naturally to us, we enter into an entirely new world" (Lewis, 2001 p. 138). When we earnestly seek God wholeheartedly, He ignites a fire within us that enables us to perceive life from His perspective and encounter His grace.

From considering something as an obligation to perceiving it as a rewarding opportunity, this profound transformation unfolds in awe-inspiring ways. Our perspective undergoes a shift that significantly impacts our actions and attitudes.

We perceive every aspect of life as a chance to serve, honour and contribute to expanding God's Kingdom. In his book "Don't Waste Your Life" author John Piper emphasizes that making a lasting impact doesn't require knowing everything but understanding the essential matters (Piper, 2003 p. 23). By prioritizing God's Kingdom above all else, we become capable of recognizing what truly matters and investing our time, talents and resources accordingly.

Seeking God's Kingdom first takes us on a journey beyond obligation and propels us into passion. As we transition from viewing things as tasks we "have to" do to perceiving them as opportunities we "get to" embrace, our lives become infused with purpose and joy. Let us cultivate a passion for all things related to God and allow His transformative power to shape our lives while impacting the world around us.

You're not abandoning the world. Instead, you are embracing the essence of heaven.

It's not about giving up on your dreams but rather enriching them with the love of God and fulfilling their purpose. When we prioritize the Kingdom of God, it's not about forsaking pursuits; it's about embracing something far more significant – the beauty of heaven itself. This profound truth can transform our lives, motivating us to strive for a purpose and fulfilling our calling.

One of the challenges we encounter while seeking God's Kingdom is being enticed by desires. The world often tempts us to find fulfilment in pleasures and material wants. However, genuine satisfaction and deep contentment can only be found through pursuing the Kingdom of God. Noted pastor and author Timothy Keller emphasizes the importance of not becoming captivated by the blessings of His Kingdom while neglecting its King. In his book "Counterfeit Gods" Keller warns against idolizing success, possessions or relationships, explaining that these things can never truly satisfy our longings.

Moreover, seeking God's Kingdom also entails embracing His love. Paul reminds us of Christ's love in his letter to the Ephesians. It encourages us to get stress and depth (Ephesians 3:18). The impact of love on our aspirations is profound, shaping them to align with God's purpose. It is through this love that we can find fulfilment and meaning. In the book "Experiencing God ", author Henry Blackaby emphasizes the importance of cultivating an intimate relationship with God as the foundation for understanding His love and purpose.

Refining our dreams through God's love and purpose is not a one; it requires humility and surrender. We must relinquish our desires and submit them to God's divine plan. In "The Pursuit of God", A.W. Tozer wisely states that reaching a point where we abandon our agendas is crucial. God's perfect plan takes shape in this place of surrender, transforming us completely.

Throughout the journey towards seeking God's Kingdom, we may encounter challenges and setbacks. However, these trials serve as opportunities for refining our dreams and strengthening our character. Joyce Meyer, an author, reminds us in her book "Battlefield of the Mind" that God's immense love for us refuses to let us remain weak or oppressed. He empowered us, enabling us to overcome obstacles and emerge stronger.

These challenges ultimately help shape us into individuals who are fully attuned to God's Kingdom and purpose in life.

When we refine our dreams through God's love and purpose, it guides us towards a life that is fulfilling and meaningful. C.S. Lewis beautifully explains this idea by suggesting that our desires aren't too intense; instead, we often settle for pleasures when infinite joy is available. By prioritizing God's Kingdom, we are not paying for anything. Instead, we embrace a reality of joy, purpose and fulfilment.

Pursuing God's Kingdom becomes an awe-inspiring journey where we seek heavenly realms and refine our dreams through His love and purpose. This profound pursuit requires surrendering our desires while aligning them with God's plan.

As we face difficulties and obstacles, we undergo a process of growth and resilience that shapes us into individuals who experience fulfilment while pursuing our calling. Therefore, let us direct our attention towards the realm of God's Kingdom, understanding that by seeking it, we are embracing the essence of heaven itself.

Chapter Two
In His Kingdom Heart

Love, Compassion and Forgiveness

Welcome to the heart of His Kingdom, where Love is our language, Compassion is our currency, and Forgiveness becomes our anthem.

Throughout my life, I've come to understand three truths that have shaped who I am and brought me immense joy and fulfilment. Love, Compassion and Forgiveness have become the guiding principles that have transformed my perspective, relationships and purpose. In this chapter of the book "In His Kingdom ", I share how these principles hold power and have taken me on an extraordinary journey.

Reflecting on my life experiences, I am reminded of the Love that has guided every step. This Love from a King goes beyond what we can comprehend. It surpasses limitations. Reaches deep into our core, awakening a longing to share this profound affection with others. It is a love that quenches the thirst in hearts and breathes life into weary souls.

Love as a Language, Compassion is the currency and Forgiveness is the anthem.

Love serves as a language that transcends barriers and unites hearts. It has become the essence of my existence. Through passion, I've learned to appreciate the beauty in every individual, embrace diversity, and forge deep connections. Love has taught me that kindness, empathy and understanding are essential in unlocking our potential and helping others thrive. Through passion, we find the courage to uplift others, lend a helping hand, and create a world where Compassion prevails.

In His Kingdom, Compassion is the currency of an act of selflessness that goes beyond our comfort zones. It speaks volumes through empathy, understanding and an authentic desire to lighten the burdens carried by others. As we fully immerse ourselves in Compassion's currency, we realize that genuine wealth isn't about material possessions. Instead, it lies in our influence and impact on the lives of those around us.

Throughout my journey, I've gathered a wealth of life experiences that have shaped me into the person I am today. But one vital lesson always stands out when I reflect on my path: true wealth isn't measured by what we own but by our effect on others' lives.

Compassion is a currency for the soul, drastically shifting my perception of the world around me. Through Compassion, we acknowledge the struggles and pain endured by others. It is through this Compassion that we gather strength to alleviate suffering.

I've come to understand that genuine wealth isn't found in material possessions but rather in our ability to extend a helping hand to those in need. By nurturing Compassion within ourselves, we can witness its impact on both the giver and the receiver. Compassion has shown me that we are all connected, and by uplifting others, we encourage ourselves.

Growing up, I often longed for symbols of success. However, it was during my adult years when reality hit me like a bolt of lightning. Volunteering at church exposed me to individuals who lacked material wealth. Possessed hearts filled with immeasurable kindness.

Their stories of resilience and hope deeply resonated with me. Made me re-evaluate my priorities. It gradually became clear that true abundance lies in how we impact others' lives. From that moment, I committed myself to building meaningful connections and making a positive difference.

Whether supporting a friend in need or helping a stranger find or give them food and accommodation, I've discovered that the valuable thing we can offer is the ability to inspire, encourage and support those around us. I witnessed others grow to find their chosen pathway and or ministry. I find that meaningful to the Kingdom of God. If that's the only currency I have, but it's available to offer, I will continue doing it to promote the money of His Kingdom, Compassion. Seeing others develop their hope through God-given and use me as an instrument for that currency of Compassion and reignite within them.

Over time, I've realized that our impact on others' lives creates a legacy beyond possessions. The happiness we experience from giving and making a difference is truly invaluable. It's not about how much money or possessions we have; instead, it's about the deep connection we feel within our souls.

So, I urge all of you fellow travellers on this journey of life to shift your focus from accumulating wealth to embracing your power in influencing others. Take a moment to reflect on the lives you've touched and the shared smiles you've exchanged. The inspiration you've provided. By doing so, you'll realize that true richness lies not in what we own but in our profound impact on people's hearts.

In a world often consumed by bitterness and resentment, Forgiveness becomes an anthem embodying the essence of His Kingdom. It's like a melody that breaks through barriers of hostility and allows our spirits to soar freely towards new horizons.

Forgiveness should not be seen as a sign of weakness but rather as a demonstration of strength. It possesses the ability to mend broken relationships and promote healing.

The transformative aspect of my journey has been embracing Forgiveness as a liberating anthem. Through Forgiveness, we let go of anger, resentment and pain, allowing healing and personal growth to unfold. It's important to note that Forgiveness is not a sign of weakness; instead, it is a testament to our strength and resilience. We free ourselves from the weight of the past and open up space for hope. Embrace the present moment. Forgiveness has taught me that releasing grudges creates room for Love, Compassion and joy to flourish.

To truly grasp the nature of His Kingdom, it is essential to seek wisdom from Biblical scholars and Christian writers who have dedicated their lives to unravelling the mysteries of divinity. John MacArthur, a respected theologian, reminds us that "love is the ultimate embodiment of God's character and lies at the core of His Kingdom" (MacArthur, 57). By embracing this Love and allowing it to flow through us, we become vessels for His presence, illuminating the darkest corners of our world.

Moreover, in his book "Love Does" (Goff, 23), Bob Goff emphasizes the significance of living a life driven by Love and Compassion. He challenges us to engage with our surroundings and serve as ambassadors for a compassionate Creator who desires to establish His Kingdom on Earth just as it is in Heaven.

As we delve deeper into comprehending the essence of His Kingdom, we begin to understand its impact on every aspect of our lives. Our perception changes, our priorities align with eternity, and our purpose becomes intertwined with His will. Life is not simply a journey from birth to death anymore; it transforms into a captivating tapestry that intricately interweaves life's stories, forming a masterpiece brimming with Love, empathy and Forgiveness.

My life's journey is evidence of Love in the language of Compassion acting as valuable currency and Forgiveness resonating as an empowering anthem. These principles have entirely transformed my perspective on life by enabling me to view the world through empathy, understanding and acceptance.

I've learned that embracing these principles can impact others, motivating them to follow suit. Let's all work towards making Love our way of communication, Compassion our way of exchange, and Forgiveness our way of expression. Doing this can create a truly inspiring and supportive world for everyone.

Embrace transformative practices that nurture love, compassion, and forgiveness.

In a world often marked by discord, division and self-interests, we must nurture Love, Compassion and Forgiveness within our communities. As individuals handpicked by God to mirror His Kingdom's values, we are responsible for initiating actions that promote these virtues. By seeking inspiration from teachings and insights shared by Bible scholars and Christian writers alike, we can wholeheartedly embrace transformative practices that nurture Love, Compassion, and Forgiveness while striving for harmony in our communities under the guidance of God.

At the core of community building lies the bedrock of Love. The Apostle Paul eloquently portrays Love as a virtue in 1 Corinthians 13:13. To create a culture of Love within our communities, we can strive to mirror the Love exemplified by Jesus Christ. By embracing the idea of "agape" love, which seeks the well-being of others, we foster an environment that values, accepts and celebrates individuals for who they are. As Charles Swindoll eloquently says, "We should free our love from the constraints of selfishness."

In 1 Corinthians 13:13, the Apostle Paul reminds us that Love is a virtue. It serves as the bedrock on which we can build a community. Love knows no boundaries; it transcends words and bridges differences to cultivate unity. As we strive to reflect God's Kingdom, let us weave Love into every thread of our lives. Sarah Young beautifully states in "Jesus Calling," "Love others just as I have loved you, even if it means sacrificing your desires for their well-being." This selfless Love breaks down barriers. Enables us to form deep connections that nurture a community marked by genuine care and Compassion.

Compassion empowers us to empathize with others and extend a helping hand. It urges us to step outside our comfort zones and reach out to those in need, following in Jesus' footsteps during his time on Earth.

To cultivate Compassion, we can support community service projects, volunteering opportunities or mentoring programs. The words of Mother Teresa serve as a source of inspiration, reminding us to make a difference, even if it's in just one person's life. When we extend our help to those on the outskirts and those who face oppression, we embody the nature exemplified by Christ. Creating an environment that fosters care and empathy is crucial.

Jesus demonstrated the essence of Compassion through His ministry, revealing its potential for transformative change. Kindness goes beyond sympathy or empathy; it requires taking tangible actions to alleviate suffering and address the needs of others. In Matthew 9:36, it is mentioned that Jesus was "moved with compassion" upon seeing the crowds, emphasizing the significance of caring for others. Mother Teresa, renowned for her acts of Compassion, beautifully expressed this sentiment when she said, "If you judge people, you have no time to love them." By setting aside judgment and wholeheartedly embracing empathy, we can establish a community where everyone feels acknowledged, valued and supported.

Forgiveness plays a role in liberating ourselves from the burden of hatred and resentment. As followers in His Kingdom's footsteps, we must embrace Forgiveness as an anthem that resounds throughout our communities. Understanding the impact of Forgiveness empowers us to initiate healing programs, support groups, and share personal stories that inspire individuals to let go of past hurts and extend grace to others just as they have experienced it themselves. C.S. Lewis reminds us that "true Forgiveness means forgiving the unforgivable because God has forgiven what was considered unforgivable in us."

Forgiveness, though challenging, possesses a power that transcends all limits. As followers of Christ, we are called to forgive as we have been forgiven (Colossians 3:13). Forgiveness brings healing and restoration to both the wrongdoer and the wounded. It fosters a community where wounds can heal and relationships can be restored. Corrie ten Boom, a Holocaust survivor who shared her wisdom in her book "The Hiding Place ", said, "Forgiveness is a choice; it can be done irrespective of one's emotional state." Choosing Forgiveness shapes our character and cultivates a community where restoration and healing thrive.

To build communities that reflect God's Kingdom, we must actively engage in initiatives that promote Love, Compassion and Forgiveness. By embracing practices rooted in wisdom and incorporating teachings from esteemed Christian authors, we can inspire and uplift one another on the journey towards cultivating these virtues.

Let's consider the words from Galatians 5:22-23; "But the fruits of the Spirit are love, joy, peace, patience, kindness, goodness, faithfulness, gentleness and self-control; against things there is no law." May our communities thrive with Love, empathy and the ability to forgive. These qualities should guide us in a world that desperately needs intervention. To create a community where passion, Compassion, and Forgiveness flourish, we must begin by looking within ourselves and embodying these virtues.

Bringing about change within our communities requires acts of Love, empathy and Forgiveness that come from deep within our hearts. As we engage with Scripture and absorb the wisdom shared by scholars and Christian authors, we will find abundant guidance to revitalize our communities.

When we embrace Love as our expression, offer empathy as the foundation for interacting with others, and make Forgiveness a fundamental aspect of all situations. We genuinely reflect God's Kingdom on Earth. Through these actions, we can bring hope, healing and reconciliation to those around us. Making an impact on our communities. Let us always remember Apostle Paul's words; "And over all these virtues put on love which binds them all in perfect unity" (Colossians 3:14).

In this memoir, I want to share my journey with the essence of His Kingdom. It's the moments that humbled me and the victories that propelled me forward. May this book kindle your fire and awaken a deep longing to embrace this divine Love, practice Compassion in all your interactions, and recognize the transformative power of Forgiveness.

Love is more than an emotion, it has the ability to touch hearts deeply.

Exploring how Love can be translated into actions that positively impact people's daily lives is a moving and inspiring conversation. Passion lies at the core of God's commandments and teachings, reflecting His nature while empowering us to create change in our surroundings.

In the Gospel of Matthew, Jesus shares his teachings on these commandments; "You shall love the Lord your God with all your heart, soul and mind" along with "You shall love your neighbour as yourself" (Matthew 22:37-39 NIV). These commandments emphasize the connection between our Love for God and our Love for others. They remind us that our commitment to God should translate into actions that impact those around us.

To manifest this essence of Love, it is crucial to grasp its depth and significance. The Greek term utilized for Love is "agape," which embodies affection that seeks the welfare and benefit of others. This Love surpasses feelings or circumstances; it involves choosing kindness, Compassion, Forgiveness and mercy.

God's boundless Love for humanity is a blueprint for how we're called to demonstrate affection towards others. In his writings, the apostle John conveys that Love cannot be solely defined by our respect for God but rather by God's Love for us, exemplified through His Son's sacrificial sending to atone for our sins (1 John 4:10, NIV). This self-sacrifice, where Jesus gave his life for our sins, is a testament to God's Love towards us. As we strive to exhibit Love towards others, we must mirror this Love and be willing to offer ourselves for their well-being.

John Stott, a biblical scholar, emphasized the significance of understanding Love as an action rather than solely an emotional sentiment. He mentioned that true Love transcends emotions; it encompasses a constant longing for the utmost well-being and goodness of the individuals we hold dear to the best of our abilities. This viewpoint serves as a reminder that authentic Love is not passive but actively seeks the welfare of others.

To truly make a difference in the lives of those around us, our expressions of Love should extend beyond our circle of family and friends. It should encompass not only our neighbours and colleagues but also strangers. Jesus exemplified this principle through his parable about the Good Samaritan, illustrating that genuine Love knows no boundaries and compels us to assist those in need (Luke 10:25-37).

John Stotts emphasized the importance of Love as an action in his writings. Similarly, Christian writer Henri Nouwen reflected on the significance of seeking and advocating for those who suffer from injustice. Nouwen emphasized that true Compassion goes beyond proximity; it requires immersing ourselves in their pain, anguish and struggles.

To translate Love into action, we must purposefully and wholeheartedly commit to living according to God's commandments. This means listening to the needs of others, empathizing with their challenges, and actively seeking ways to alleviate their burdens. As the apostle Paul wrote in Philippians 2:3-4 (NIV), we are called to set our self-centred ambitions and conceit. Instead, we should prioritize others above ourselves. Genuinely care about their interests rather than solely focusing on our own desires. This verse encourages us to exemplify Christ's Love by prioritizing the well-being of others.

Every day presents us with opportunities to weave a narrative of Love that positively impacts those around us. Through acts of kindness and service, we can become channels through which God's grace flows and contributes meaningfully to our communities. As renowned Christian writer Brennan Manning wisely observed, "Every interaction we have with someone holds the power either to uplift or deplete them; there is no exchange. "It is essential for us to purposefully shape a narrative that inspires and influences others through our actions while embodying the true essence of Love as guided by the divine realm.

Love knows No boundaries

When we contemplate the idea that Love within the realm knows no limits and includes all beings, we cannot help but be awestruck by the infinite capacity of God's Love for us. This realization is profound and transformative, urging us to practice this boundless Love in our daily lives regardless of societal divisions or biases.

One of the truths revealed in Scripture is that God is Love (1 John 4:8). Love isn't simply an attribute associated with God; it defines His nature. His Love isn't restricted to a few or hindered by prejudices; it goes beyond human comprehension and encompasses all aspects of creation. As we meditate on this truth, we understand that our ability to love stems not from our strength alone but from the boundless Love emanating from God Himself.

In his book "Mere Christianity ", C.S. Lewis beautifully explores the concept of Love within Christianity. He articulates that Christian Love, whether directed towards God or humans, is an act of the will. It's not merely a feeling of affection but a conscious decision to act lovingly, even towards those we may consider undeserving. Lewis eloquently highlights this idea by emphasizing that Love goes beyond sentiment and calls us to step out of our comfort zones and societal divisions, embracing Love for all beings just as God does.

Another thought-provoking perspective on the practice of Love comes from N.T. Wright, a Bible scholar. In his book "Surprised by Hope" Wright emphasizes the transformative power of Love in breaking down societal barriers. He argues that the Kingdom of God is characterized by an encompassing and inclusive love that surpasses prejudices and bridges societal gaps. Wright encourages participation in bringing about this Kingdom through acts of Love and service as they provide glimpses into the reality that awaits us all.

Living out Love can be challenging in a world where division and prejudices are often promoted. However, Scripture guides us to resist conforming to these patterns but rather be transformed by renewing our minds (Romans 12:2). When we deeply engage with the teachings of God's Word, we gain a perspective on Love.

In his book "The Way of the Heart ", theologian Henri Nouwen shares insights. Nouwen encourages us to embrace moments of solitude and prayer, allowing God's Love to profoundly touch our hearts. He emphasizes that it is after experiencing God's transformative Love that we can truly love others without limitations. Nouwen reminds us that boundless Love originates from our transformation as we draw closer to God and allow His overflowing Love to manifest through us.

Love in the Kingdom of God knows no boundaries, which is awe-inspiring. As we actively practice this Love in our lives, disregarding divisions and biases, we find inspiration and wisdom from esteemed Bible scholars and Christian authors, like C.S. Lewis, N.T. Wright and Henri Nouwen. They remind us that Love is not an emotion but a conscious choice that leads to personal transformation. We can extend God's Love to every being through prayer, studying God's Word, and renewing our minds.

One effective routine that aids in nurturing and cultivating Love, Compassion and Forgiveness within us is prayer. Through prayer, we open our hearts to divine presence while seeking guidance and transformation. As Matthew Henry once noted as a Bible scholar, "Prayer will. Make a person cease from sin or sin will entice them to cease from prayer." Prayer serves as a way to connect with God, allowing Him to work in our lives by softening our hearts and helping us grow in the qualities of the Spirit. Besides prayer, it is crucial to meditate on Scripture to develop Love, Compassion and Forgiveness. The Bible is a source of wisdom and guidance that acts like a compass for navigating life's challenges.

In his letter to the Colossians, the apostle Paul emphasized the importance of embracing Christ's teachings and letting them profoundly influence our lives. This entails gaining wisdom and knowledge from the Word while encouraging and guiding one another through psalms, hymns and spiritual songs with hearts filled with grace for the Lord (Colossians 3:16, KJV). When we immerse ourselves in God's Word, we allow ourselves to be transformed and better equipped to show others love, Compassion and Forgiveness.

Cultivating an attitude of gratitude plays a role in nurturing personal growth. By focusing on being grateful, we train our hearts to appreciate the blessings in our lives rather than dwelling on grievances or shortcomings. Ann Voskamp, an author, beautifully captures the essence of this concept in her book "One Thousand Gifts." She emphasizes that gratitude is not only a virtue but also the very foundation for all other virtues. Embracing gratitude allows Love to flourish by redirecting our focus from ourselves and towards the goodness that surrounds us. This creates a ground for Compassion and Forgiveness to take root within our hearts.

Nurture and cultivate Love, Compassion and Forgiveness within us. It is crucial to embody the teachings of Christ in all our interactions with others. As mentioned by the apostle Peter in his letter, we should strive to adopt a mindset of empathy and Love for one another and display acts of Compassion and humility (1 Peter 3:8 NIV). By incorporating Love and kindness into our lives, we live out Christ's teachings and extend understanding and Forgiveness to those around us.

Integrating prayer, studying Scripture, expressing gratitude, and genuinely and intentionally practising acts of love and kindness impact nurturing and cultivating Love, Compassion and Forgiveness within our hearts. Through these habits, we open ourselves to God's transformative power as He moulds us into vessels that reflect His Love and grace.

Above all, let us place our trust in the ability of God to nurture and develop these qualities within us. As the apostle Paul said with conviction, "I am certain that God, who initiated this work within you will continue His work until it is ultimately completed on the day Christ Jesus returns" (Philippians 1:6 NIV). May our hearts serve as the soil where Love, Compassion and Forgiveness are sown like seeds. May they flourish into blessings that bring glory to God.

Compassion is like a glimpse into the depths of humanity.

Compassion intertwines with our existence, empowering us to create a divine presence here on Earth. In those moments when we witness Compassion in action, we catch a glimpse of the Holy working through us. One particular memory remains etched vividly, forever inspiring me with its impact.

On a wintry night, I found myself amidst the bustling streets of a city surrounded by those who have been marginalized and forgotten. Among them stood a woman, her frail figure trembling against the wind. As I approached her, my heart swelled with both empathy and unease. However, a stranger emerged from the crowd at that moment—a face I had never seen before emanating warmth that seemed to defy the wintry chill.

With hands, this kind-hearted individual extended a blanket to the woman—an act of Compassion that completely transformed her demeanour. Her eyes, once filled with despair, now shimmered with hope. In that instant, I witnessed Compassion's incredible power as it provided physical comfort and ignited a flicker of dignity deep within her soul.

This profound encounter left a mark on my Spirit, a constant reminder of our divine duty to love and care for one another. As a renowned biblical scholar, Matthew Henry eloquently wrote, "Compassion can mend sins in ways that condemnation never could." At that moment, I realized that Compassion could heal wounds, mend brokenness, and bridge even the widest gaps that separate us.

Henri Nouwen, an author who truly captures the essence of Compassion, beautifully expresses its nature when he states, "Compassion impels us to step into places of pain and embrace brokenness, fear, confusion and anguish. It challenges us to stand in solidarity with those suffering, mourning alongside them and shedding tears for their sorrows." Witnessing acts of Compassion did not just affect the woman in need but also touched the hearts of all who were fortunate enough to see it. It served as a reminder that we're vessels of God's Love and are responsible for showing Compassion towards those who are hurting and marginalized. These displays of empathy taught us that by making His Kingdom visible here on Earth, we become conduits for grace.

Unity thrives through the coexistence of elements.

God's Kingdom unity does not stem from everyone's being. Instead, it arises from the differences present in His creation. By embracing our individuality, we foster a sense of respect and inclusivity that flourishes amidst the complexities of our world. The story of a knit community exemplifies how unity in diversity can bring about positive change. Within this community, individuals with backgrounds, cultures, and perspectives came together because they shared a love for God and one another. They understood that genuine unity does not require conformity; instead, it calls for ears, a willingness to learn from others and an appreciation for each person's unique contributions.

In their gatherings for worship, they would sing songs that blended melodies from cultures, creating a harmonious symphony of praise. When they read scriptures together, they found wisdom in the interpretations and insights shared by their fellow believers. During conversations and discussions, they engaged respectfully with one another to seek understanding rather than trying to persuade or convince others.

This community embraced the teachings of the apostle Paul, who wrote, "There is no distinction between Jew or Greek, slave or free person, male or female; you are all one in Christ Jesus" (Galatians 3:28). Recognizing and embracing diversity among them was seen as essential for fostering unity as it revealed the beauty of Gods Kingdom, in his book "Surprised by Hope ", renowned biblical scholar N.T. Wright emphasizes the importance of cultivating inclusivity and mutual respect within Christ's body, showcasing the Gospel's power.

Richard J. Mouw, an author and theologian, echoes this sentiment by emphasizing the importance of engaging in conversations while holding our convictions with humility and grace. In his book "Uncommon Decency; Christian Civility in an Uncivil World ", Mouw explores the idea of unity amid diversity, emphasizing the importance for believers to cultivate respect and understanding when confronted with disagreements.

Through their dedication to inclusivity and respect, this knit community became a beacon of hope in a world often divided by fear and prejudice. Their example encourages us to embrace our differences, listen with empathy, and celebrate the tapestry of God's creation. By doing so, we can become catalysts for harmony, reflecting the Love and kindness of our Divine Creator.

Forgiveness holds power within the Kingdom of God.

When we deeply contemplate Forgiveness, we discover it is a key that unlocks our liberation. By forgiving others, we release ourselves from the burdens that weigh us down and create space for the power of divine mercy. This truth compels us to examine areas where Forgiveness can be generously extended, leading to healing and restoration.

One significant domain where Forgiveness finds its place is within our relationships. The theologian and writer C.S. Lewis reminds us that as Christians, part of our journey is forgiving even the seemingly unforgivable because God extends His

Forgiveness towards what was deemed unforgivable in ourselves. In his book "The Weight of Glory ", Lewis emphasizes the importance of developing Forgiveness for those who have wronged us, reflecting God's act of Forgiveness towards all.

Within a family, Forgiveness can mend bonds and restore harmony. The apostle Paul encourages us to bear with one another and forgive any grievances that may arise among us. We are called upon to extend Forgiveness just as the Lord has forgiven us (Colossians 3:13). Embracing Forgiveness in our relationships fosters an atmosphere where Love, understanding and reconciliation can thrive within our homes.

When forgiving ourselves, we often carry the burden of mistakes and regrets. However, the psalmist reminds us of the truth: our transgressions are entirely removed from us just as the East is distant from the West (Psalm 103:12). Forgiveness does not just benefit others but also us and those we encounter in our communities. In "The Art of Forgiving ", Lewis B. Smedes explains that Forgiveness releases a prisoner only to realize that we are alone. When we choose Forgiveness, we liberate ourselves from resentment and bitterness, experiencing freedom to live authentically and wholeheartedly.

The life and teachings of Jesus Christ serve as an example of Forgiveness. As he hung on the cross, he uttered these words; "Father, forgive them for they do not know what they are doing" (Luke 23:34). Through his sacrifice, Jesus demonstrated how Forgiveness can redeem lives and bring about transformative change. When we contemplate that Forgiveness is crucial for freeing our souls, it prompts us to consider areas where we can practice Forgiveness more generously. Whether it involves forgiving others or seeking Forgiveness from God, choosing to ignore opens the path to healing, renewal and a profound encounter with God's Love.

Our genuine power resides in the unity found within our spirits.

Our genuine power resides in the unity found within our spirits. Each person is uniquely moulded by a force with their talents, gifts and life experiences. When we embrace and honour this diversity, we can seamlessly weave together a tapestry fuelled by Love and understanding.

The apostle Paul reminds us in his letter to the Corinthians that although there are kinds of gifts, they all originate from the same source (1 Corinthians 12:4). This biblical wisdom emphasizes how diverse contributions within Christ's body enrich our unity and how colours and patterns enhance a tapestry. In his book "The Living Church ", Christian writer and theologian John Stott encourages us to embrace diversity as a reflection of God's creativity. He explains that the church should be more than a gathering of like-minded individuals; instead, it is a divinely crafted community composed of diverse individuals who have found reconciliation with God and each other. Acknowledging and valuing these differences creates an environment where everyone can thrive and contribute to society.

As we aim for unity amidst diversity, we must refrain from judging or excluding those different from us. The Apostle Paul, in his letter to the Galatians, reminds us that in Christ Jesus, there are no distinctions based on ethnicity (Jew or Gentile), social status (slave or free) or gender (male or female) (Galatians 3:28). This inspiring truth from the Bible encourages us to break down the barriers that separate us and instead come together as equals recognizing our shared humanity.

When we truly value and celebrate our diversity, it creates a tapestry of harmony that reflects God's wisdom. By appreciating each person's contributions, seeking understanding, and embracing unity, we can experience a life enriched by the abundance of Christ. In Love and Compassion, we discover that resonates from a place. Every small act sets off a chain reaction of affection and empathy worldwide.

In a world often marked by turmoil and division, our simple acts of Love and kindness hold the power to ignite a chain reaction that spreads God's divine Love and Compassion. When we purposefully choose to show Love, we can inspire others profoundly and make an impact that heals our world.

In his book "The Return of the Prodigal Son ", Henri Nouwen, a theologian and author, beautifully conveys the profound influence of Love. He reminds us that through acts of Love, we create something new that didn't exist before we shared it with others. It is essential to remember that seemingly insignificant gestures of Love possess the potential to create far-reaching ripples beyond what we can immediately perceive.

In the Gospel of Matthew, the Bible encourages us to let our inner light shine before others so that they may witness our deeds and give glory to our Heavenly Father (Matthew 5:16). This passage serves as a reminder that acts of Love and kindness are never in vain; instead, they have the power to inspire others and bring them closer to God.

In his book "Outlive Your Life ", Max Lucado, an author and pastor, urges us to lead a life filled with Love that leaves a lasting impact. He emphasizes that acts of kindness and Love can be like a wave of grace unleashed by God rather than just small ripples created by throwing a pebble into a pond.

To ensure that our small acts of kindness have the desired impact, we must cultivate a heart of Compassion and Love. In his letter to the Colossians (Colossians 3:12), the apostle Paul encourages us to embrace qualities such as Compassion, kindness, humility, gentleness and patience. When we consciously embody these qualities, we become ambassadors of God's Love and Compassion.

Mother Teresa, a Christian figure recognized for her acts of Compassion, once wisely stated, "While we may not all possess the ability to achieve monumental feats, we can certainly make a difference through small gestures performed with great love." Through these expressions of kindness and affection, we hold the power to make a significant impact on those around us.

When we ensure that our acts of goodwill and tenderness are rooted in the Love of God and guided by His wisdom, we can trust that they will leave an enduring imprint on our society. By extending Love and Compassion to others, we become vessels of God's grace, sharing His Love and offering hope to those in need.

Remember that each demonstration of Love, every act of Compassion, and every instance of Forgiveness carries an influence far beyond our imagination. It originates from within us. Reaches out to touch lives in ways that surpass our understanding. This is the heart of God's Kingdom.

Chapter Three
In His Kingdom Identity

Discovering Our True Identity

Living in a world filled with division, hatred and arrogance, it becomes crucial for believers to humbly embrace our identity within the kingdom. This isn't some abstract idea; it's a life-altering reality that originates from God's heart. As we embark on this journey towards fully embracing our identity in the kingdom, we are called to mirror the character of Christ Himself – being humble, loving and inclusive.

The Scriptures serve as a guide on this path towards embracing our authentic identity within the kingdom. In Philippians, the Apostle Paul reminds us not to act out of ambition or conceit but rather show humility by considering others as more significant than ourselves. We are encouraged to look beyond our interests and genuinely care about the well-being of others (Philippians 2:3-4 ESV). This powerful message establishes a foundation for us to pursue humility. It emphasizes that to truly embrace our identity in the kingdom, we must let go of selfishness and prioritize others above ourselves.

In his book "Paul and the Gift ", Professor John Barclay, a known expert in Bible studies, delves deeper into this concept. Barclay emphasizes that God's grace goes beyond being undeserved favour – it is also a transformative force that empowers us to live according to our true identity in the kingdom. He eloquently explains that grace does not pardon and acquit but also bestows honour and status upon its recipients. This has social implications, such as fostering humility, gratitude and generosity (Barclay 126). Through his insights, Barclay invites us to understand that embracing our kingdom identity is not a self-centred pursuit; instead, it compels us to honour others by acknowledging the grace we have received.

Donna Schaper takes up the mantle in her book, "Radical Hospitality," where she challenges Christians to wholeheartedly embrace diversity. She paints a picture of how diversity is integral to our kingdom's identity. According to Schaper, hospitality is more than an action; it is a way of thinking and feeling that seeks inclusion rather than exclusion. Then, perceiving differences as threats, we can view them as opportunities for growth and connection with others – approaching these encounters with openness and love (Schaper 41).

Schaper invites us to embrace the tapestry of cultures, races and backgrounds that intertwine in our world. Through diversity, we can indeed. Experience the beauty of God's creation.

Embracing our identity within the kingdom requires a love beyond societal barriers. The Apostle Paul reminds us in his letter to the Galatians that what matters is not factors like circumcision or uncircumcision but rather faith expressed through love (Galatians 5;6 ESV). This essential truth shows that our primary identity lies in Christ, and our faith is demonstrated by our love for one another. Honey is a bond that unites us regardless of our differences, enabling us to live out our kingdom identity purposefully.

Our journey towards embracing our kingdom identity with humility, love and a celebration of diversity may be challenging. However, as we immerse ourselves in Scripture's wisdom and learn from scholars and authors, we gain valuable tools to embark on this transformative path. Let us wholeheartedly embrace our kingdom identity inspired by Christ's character and rooted in humility while being fuelled by love.

Bringing their unique perspectives and gifts to the world.

Understanding our identity in Christ is a meaningful concept at the heart of the Christian faith. It speaks to the impact of God's love and grace as it establishes believers as children of God who have been forgiven and redeemed through Jesus Christ's sacrifice. However, when considering individuals' intricate identities beyond their religious beliefs, we must acknowledge the potential for exclusion or marginalization from prioritizing only one religious identity.

It is crucial to approach this subject with humility, empathy and a genuine willingness to engage with perspectives. The Bible teaches us that all individuals are created in God's image (Genesis 1:27) and that Jesus himself embraced and reached out to those society had marginalized. As followers of Christ, we are called to extend this love and acceptance to all people regardless of their religious beliefs or identities.

According to N.T. Wright, a known expert on the Bible, states that our identity in Christ doesn't mean that other identities lose value or importance. Instead, it means we should appreciate and celebrate the diversity of God's creation. We should recognize that each person brings unique perspectives and gifts. Wright emphasizes that "Understanding our Identity in Christ doesn't erase identities but redefines them within the context of God's love and redemption" (Wright, 2016).

Acknowledging that prioritizing one identity over others can lead to exclusion or marginalization is crucial. However, this contradicts the teachings of Christ. In his letter to the Galatians, the apostle Paul reminds us that in Christ, there is no distinction between Jew or Greek, slave or free, male or female (Galatians 3:28). This verse highlights how inclusive the Gospel is. It challenges us to go beyond divisions by embracing those who may be different from us. By doing so, we actively work against any potential exclusion or marginalization caused by prioritizing just one religious' identity.

Christian writer Anne Lamott beautifully captures this sentiment when she expresses, "It's a telling sign that we've created God in our image when it turns out that God despises the same people we do" (Lamott, 1999). This reminds us of the importance of not prioritizing one identity over others, as doing so can distort the true essence of God's love.

To navigate these complexities effectively, engaging in meaningful conversations while actively listening is crucial. By seeking to comprehend and accept the diverse identities of individuals, we can establish inclusive and loving environments. As Timothy Keller, another author, emphasizes, "Love is the most sacred and powerful action in the universe. Love encompasses all virtues; it is what Christ truly desires us to embody and what sin perpetually opposes" (Keller, 2013).

Reconciling the idea of Understanding our Identity in Christ with individuals' varied identities beyond their religious beliefs necessitates a sensitive and empathetic approach. By acknowledging the value of each person, extending love and empathy towards them, and actively opposing exclusion and marginalization, we can foster a more inclusive and empathetic society.

As followers of Christ, let us wholeheartedly embrace the beautiful diversity that God has woven into His creation and extend His boundless love to every individual, regardless of their religious beliefs or personal characteristics.

View yourselves through the lens of God's love.

Discovering ourselves by perceiving ourselves through the lens of God's profound love requires navigating through a world filled with diverse and sometimes conflicting perspectives. In today's society, where there is a tendency to define our identities based on gender, sexual orientation, race, social status and other labels, it becomes essential for us as believers to comprehend our role in this world and how God's love moulds our genuine identity.

The relentless barrage of messages from the world often attempts to shape us into a meld, leaving us feeling inadequate and adrift. However, the Scriptures assure us that our true identity does not lie in these factors but in our intimate connection with God. In his book "The Freedom of Self Forgetfulness", Timothy Keller, a known Christian author, highlights the significance of reflecting on the profound reversals we experience. It's a realization that we're more flawed and sinful than we could have ever imagined but, at the same time, more accepted and loved than we dared to hope.

The world often limits our understanding of identity by shifting with societal norms and expectations. However, God's perspective is unchanging and eternal. In his letter to the Ephesians, the apostle Paul reminds us that we are God's masterpiece. Christ Jesus has given us a beginning to fulfil the good plans He had for us since long ago (Ephesians 2:10 NLT). Our true identity is deeply rooted in God's creation, with each of us having a purpose.

John Piper, another author in his book "Desiring God" emphasizes this truth by stating that God is most glorified when our satisfaction lies in Him. Our identity shouldn't be sought after through pleasures or worldly recognition; instead, it should come from finding contentment in God's love and His purpose for our lives.

When we align our hopes and aspirations with Him, we unlock a sense of fulfilment that the world can never provide.

God's love allows us to reconcile the contrasting viewpoints of society and comprehend our role within it. Noted theologian Henri Nouwen, in his book "Life of the Beloved" reminds us that "Embracing our beloved means allowing the truth of being loved to manifest in all our thoughts, words and actions." When we fully embrace the truth that God loves us deeply, our sense of self becomes secure despite any judgments or expectations from the world.

Moreover, Jesus Himself offers wisdom and guidance on discovering our identity. In Matthew 10:39, Jesus states, "Those who cling to their life will lose it; those who let go for my sake will find life" (NIV). By surrendering our desires and aligning ourselves with God's divine purpose, we uncover a truly abundant existence and an authentic identity rooted in Him.

Our identity through the lens of God's love necessitates reconciling the diverse and conflicting perspectives prevalent in society. By recognizing that our uniqueness stems from our relationship with God, we can resist society's attempts to define us based on criteria. Then, seeking satisfaction and purpose elsewhere, we discover true fulfilment by aligning ourselves with the will of God and embracing His love for us. As we embark on this journey of self-discovery, let us remember the words of the apostle Paul in Romans 12:2; "Do not conform to the ways of this world but let your mind be transformed. Then you will be able to discern and embrace God-pleasing and perfect will" (NIV).

Our identity in Christ is not a goal to strive for; it is a spiritual reality.

Our identity in Christ and life's challenges requires perseverance, faith and surrendering control to God. Our identity in Christ is not determined by circumstances but rooted in the unchanging truth found in God's Word (Ephesians 2:10). We are fearfully and wonderfully created with a purpose by our loving Creator.

When faced with difficulties, fix your gaze upon Jesus – He is our faith's source guiding us towards perfection (Hebrews 12:2).

In his book "The Problem of Pain ", C.S. Lewis reminds us that during times of pain, we can hear the voice of God loud and clear, urging us to place our trust in Him and reminding us of who we are (Lewis, 91).

Remember to cast all your worries onto God because He genuinely cares for you (1 Peter 5:7). Jerry Bridges, in his work "Trusting God When Life Hurts", highlights the importance of choosing a more positive response when faced with hardships (Bridges, 34). Embracing our identity in Christ means having faith that God is working all things together for our good (Romans 8:28).

In his book "Walking with God Through Pain and Suffering", Timothy Keller offers insights by emphasizing the path towards joy, life, freedom and hope through embracing challenges (Keller, 265).

Our identity in Christ and life's difficulties can feel overwhelming. However, immersing ourselves in the wisdom shared by Bible scholars and Christian authors provides inspiration and godly guidance to keep our faith grounded. By keeping our identity in Christ at heart, fixing our gaze on Jesus, and entrusting our worries to God while trusting His divine plan, we confidently navigate this tension with unwavering faith. As we grasp hold of and embrace our identity rooted in Christ's love for us, we gain strength to face any adversity, knowing that we are never alone; moreover, we find solace in the assurance that God works all things together for our well-being.

Accepting Christ isn't just turning a page.

In our pursuit of growth, accepting Christ as our saviour is the beginning of a lifelong journey towards transformation. It goes beyond changing locations or starting a narrative; it invites us to live lives authored entirely by God Himself. As Christians, we should strive for transformation where every chapter in our lives reflects God's boundless wisdom, grace and love.

To ensure that experiencing a transformation through accepting Christ, nurturing a deep connection with God is crucial. This connection goes beyond attending church services or reciting prayers; it entails fostering an intimate and personal bond with the divine. Dallas Willard, a scholar of the Bible, emphasized this point when he stated, "The essence of the gospel lies not only in entering the Kingdom of Heaven after death but also in living within its realm even before death" (Willard, D. "The Divine Conspiracy" p. 11).

Living within the Kingdom of Heaven entails allowing God to guide our lives, as the author. It involves surrendering our plans, desires and ambitions to His divine will. In doing so, we place our trust in His plans for us, knowing that they surpass anything we could ever imagine and bring true fulfilment. As stated by the Apostle Paul in his letter to the Philippians, "I am capable of accomplishing all things through Christ who empowers me" (Philippians 4:13).

However, this profound transformation is not a one-time occurrence but a process where we continually let go of ourselves and strive to live for Christ daily. Jerry Bridges, an author who beautifully captures this truth in his book "The Pursuit of Holiness", elucidates this concept further.

He explains, "Holiness is not something we reach or achieve as a destination. Rather it's a process of personal growth and gradual change." (Bridges, J., "The Pursuit of Holiness", p. 19)

To ensure that every chapter of our lives is guided by God's hand, we must consistently seek His direction through prayer and meditation on His teachings. By immersing ourselves in the Scriptures, we uncover the principles and values that should shape our choices and behaviours. As the psalmist beautifully expressed, "Your word illuminates my path like a lamp lighting my way." (Psalm 119:105)

We must surround ourselves with believers who support and challenge us on our spiritual journey. In his book "The Meaning of Marriage ", Christian author and pastor Timothy Keller emphasizes the significance of having a community of believers. He writes, "Friendship does not emerge from being part of a community but also plays a vital role in our transformative journey." (Keller, T., "The Meaning of Marriage", p. 214)

This transformative journey has its challenges. We will inevitably encounter trials, temptations and setbacks along the way. However, we can find strength and encouragement in God's promise.

The Apostle James reminds us to find joy in trials as they test our faith and build perseverance (James 1:2-3).

Accepting Christ as our saviour should result in a transformation where every aspect of our lives is guided by God's hand. To achieve this transformation, it is vital to nurture a relationship with God, surrender our plans to align with His will, seek His guidance through prayer and Scripture study, and surround ourselves with fellow believers for support and accountability while being open to embracing the challenges that may come our way.

On the transformation journey, we discover fulfilment, joy and the abundant life God has promised us.

We are bestowed with the status of royal priests.

In the story of life, Christians are tasked with embracing a paradoxical identity. We are priests in Christ's kingdom, bearing a divine heritage and heavenly purpose. Simultaneously, we acknowledge the existence of inequality, injustice and suffering in our world. This intriguing journey challenges our perception of where we fit in society and how we contribute to God's mission of justice and love.

The concept of being royal priests originated from the Old Testament when God called upon Israel to be a priesthood (Exodus 19:6). However, this call was not exclusive to priests or leaders; it extended to the entire nation. Today, as believers in Christ, we participate in this honour as partakers in the priesthood.

In his book titled "The Divine Conspiracy", Dallas Willard asserts that the inclusion of every individual who genuinely belongs to the covenant is an outcome of Christ's work and is not limited to an exclusive group of saints. Our divine inheritance and purpose extend beyond a few; it is an open invitation to all those who have been redeemed by the sacrifice of Jesus.

Simultaneously, we must acknowledge the existence of inequality, injustice and suffering in our world. These disparities are evident in the gaps between the wealthy and the impoverished, the oppressed and oppressors, and those on society's margins versus those with privilege. This reality has persisted since humanity's fall. Continues to afflict our world today. However, as followers of Christ, we cannot remain passive in light of these challenges.

The apostle Paul reminds us in his letter to the Ephesians that our struggle is not against human beings but against rulers, authorities, dark forces in this world and spiritual evil entities in heavenly realms (Ephesians 6:12). As individuals with a calling, it is our responsibility to actively participate in the spiritual battle against the injustices that exist in the world. We aim to establish God's kingdom by standing up against these injustices. Richard Bauckham, in his book "The Theology of the Book of Revelation ", emphasizes that the Book of Revelation urges communities to engage with the real world, empowering them to bear witness, endure difficulties, and act despite facing opposition.

Although this task may appear daunting, we derive hope and encouragement from our identity in Christ. The apostle Peter reminds us that we are not just people; instead, we have been specifically chosen by God to be part of a particular group—a royal priesthood and a holy nation—His treasured possession (1 Peter 2:9). The same God who has called us into this position has also promised to equip us and give us the strength needed to fulfil our purpose. As A.W. Tozer expresses in his book "The Pursuit of God ", our lives have transformed; from being slaves or rebels, we have become trusted servants and cherished friends of God granted access to His very presence.

Our identity as priests with a divine heritage and purpose while acknowledging the existence of inequality and suffering, we must hold onto God's promises and actively advance His kingdom. This is not a task, but as we rely on Him and draw from His profound wisdom, we can discover the strength and encouragement needed to persevere.

Chosen people blessed with a purpose aligned with the kingdom's vision.

As beings, we often find ourselves navigating between two contrasting realms. On the one hand, there is the potential that comes with our unique individuality, filled with meaning and elegance. On the other hand, there is the sobering reality of our existence as survivors in a world plagued by suffering and uncertainty. Striking a balance between these two can be challenging. Still, we must explore and comprehend how to lead a fulfilling and purpose-driven life.

The Bible imparts wisdom that emphasizes how we possess a purpose and have been bestowed with grace. Ephesians 2:10 states, "For we are God's handiwork, created in Christ Jesus for works which God prepared beforehand for us to walk in." Our uniqueness is not accidental; it is a choice made by a loving Creator. Theologian NT Wright eloquently captures this notion by stating, " God's selection of us isn't random or arbitrary; it is a calling to restore His creation through love and purpose." By comprehending our chosen identity, we establish a foundation to fully embrace our potential and fulfil God's intended purpose.

While we find solace and purpose in our identity, we must acknowledge the realities of pain and uncertainty in our world. The Apostle Paul understood this balance and reminded us in Romans 8:18 that "the sufferings of today cannot be compared to the glory that will be revealed within us." A writer, Ravi Zacharias, wisely stated that amidst life's countless questions, the most crucial isn't about suffering but finding meaning. By accepting the reality of suffering, we can navigate through times and discover hope through God's promises.

As we strive to find a balance in life, seeking wisdom from a divine source becomes crucial. The book of Proverbs contains a treasure trove of insights on living. In Proverbs 3:5-6 it advises us to put our trust in the Lord and not solely rely on our own understanding. It encourages us to submit ourselves to Him in all areas of life, promising He will guide our paths straight. Renowned author C.S.

Lewis beautifully expressed his belief in Christianity, comparing it to the rising sun that illuminates everything around us. By aligning our thoughts and actions with God's wisdom, we protect ourselves from being overwhelmed by the tension between who we choose to be and the realities we face.

Throughout history, remarkable tales have emerged of individuals who triumphed over adversity and uncertainty, serving as a source of inspiration and encouragement for others. The story of Joseph in the Book of Genesis is an illustration of this concept. Despite enduring betrayal, false accusations and imprisonment, Joseph emerged as a leader and saviour. His unwavering faith in God's plan. His commitment to remaining steadfast serves as an inspiring example for us to embrace our true identity and persevere through life's challenges.

Navigating the balance between embracing our chosen identity as individuals and facing the harsh realities of a world filled with suffering and uncertainty is undoubtedly challenging. However, armed with the wisdom found in teachings and insights from esteemed Christian authors, we can discover inspiration, encouragement and a profound sense of purpose throughout this journey. By embracing our unique identities, acknowledging the existence of suffering, seeking guidance from godly wisdom, and drawing inspiration from those who have triumphed over adversity, we equip ourselves to navigate the often-tumultuous path of life. In doing we find hope, strength and comfort in knowing that our loving Creator walks alongside us every step of the way. Guiding us during times of uncertainty and offering solace during moments of distress.

True identity lies in Christ's hands. Not merely shaped by circumstances.

Amidst every struggle to define who we are as individuals, it becomes paramount to never forget that our genuine identity lies within the hands of Christ. It is not solely determined by conditions but rather intricately moulded by our divine

Creator. This powerful truth is a source of inspiration while instilling hope within us. Reassuring us that we are unconditionally loved and profoundly valued by God himself. In moments when confusion or uncertainty cloud our minds, it is all too easy to lose sight of ourselves.

However, it is essential to remember that known experts in Bible studies and Christian literature often emphasize that our actual value and purpose lie solely in our connection with Christ.

The apostle Paul, a respected figure within the Christian community, reminds us of our identity in Christ. In his letter to the Ephesians, he states, "We are God's masterpiece, created in Christ Jesus for works that He has prepared in advance for us to do" (Ephesians 2:10, ESV). Paul highlights that we are not simply products of chance or circumstance but creations of God. Our core identity is firmly rooted in Him. It is through this connection that we discover our calling and purpose. This affirmation alone should ignite inspiration, urging us to stand firm in our identity rooted in Christ.

Renowned Christian author John Piper shares insights in his book "Don't Waste Your Life ", encouraging readers to find their true identity within their relationship with Christ and the eternal impact it can have on their lives. He writes, "You were designed for something than yourself. Your identity rooted in Christ holds the key, to unlocking a life filled with meaning and purpose" (Piper, 2003, p. 87).

Piper beautifully highlights the significance of identifying ourselves as children of God. It goes beyond our existence as we are privileged to participate in God's work and bring Him glory through our lives.

Furthermore, the esteemed theologian C.S. Lewis reminds us of the power of embracing our identity in Christ. In his book "Mere Christianity" Lewis states, "Once you have fully surrendered yourself, you no longer have the ability to change on your own. Instead, you must turn to God for transformation. Through Him can you discover your true self" (Lewis, 1952 p. 75). Lewis urges us to yield our lives to Christ, recognizing that it is through Him that our authentic identity is revealed. As we let go of self-centred desires and allow God to shape us, we encounter the beauty of who we are in Him.

Our identity in Christ does not affirm our value but also assures us of God's ending love and grace. Max Lucado, an author known for his book "You Are Special ", beautifully portrays this truth by writing, "No matter how much approval or rejection we receive from others, it cannot alter the fact that we are loved and cherished by God. "Our sense of self is firmly rooted in our relationship with Christ, providing stability and strength in times of uncertainty and doubt." These profound words beautifully capture the essence of an uplifting story. A story that resonates with our core and offers hope during uncertain times. In a world where change, doubts and insecurities abound, discovering our identity in Christ is not just a matter of faith but a profound truth that can profoundly transform lives.

As we navigate the complexities of life, self-doubt often clouds our judgment. Hinders our progress. The shifting sands of doubt can quickly sweep us away, leaving us untethered and lost. During these moments, clinging to our identity in Christ becomes essential. This identity acts as an anchor, grounding us amidst the storms and providing a solid foundation for our faith as we navigate the challenges that come our way.

In the Bible, the apostle Paul reminds us of how significant it is to embrace our identity in Christ. In his letter to the Ephesians, he writes, "For we are Gods masterpiece. He has created us a new in Christ Jesus so that we may walk in the works He prepared for us long ago" (Ephesians 2:10, NLT).

This beautiful verse reflects that our sense of self in Christ is not determined by our accomplishments or abilities but by God's gracious work within us. Recognizing that we are wonderfully and fearfully created for a purpose empowers us to overcome self-doubt and pursue the deeds that God has prepared for us.

Our identity in Christ is an anchor amidst the ever-shifting sands of self-doubt. It provides stability and fortitude, empowering us to navigate life's challenges and overcome our insecurities. Drawing from Ephesians 2:10, as shared by the apostle

Paul, along with insights from esteemed Bible scholars, we are reminded of how discovering our identity in Christ holds transformative power.

It is not like a switch we can flick on or off based on circumstances.

In a world that constantly tries to shape us according to its standards, we must fully understand that our identity is firmly grounded solely in Christ. We cannot toggle our identity in Christ on and off based on circumstances. It serves as a guiding light illuminating our journey. These profound words capture the reality of our unchanging and unwavering identity in Christ, even when faced with challenges and trials.

The Bible offers verses that remind us of our true nature in Christ. Ephesians 2:10 states, "We are God's masterpiece, created in Christ Jesus for works, which God prepared beforehand so that we could walk in them." This verse beautifully portrays the idea that we're not random beings but intentional creations skillfully crafted by God. As a result, our identity is intricately interwoven with the purpose and plan God has designed for our lives.

Max Lucado, a Christian author and speaker, emphasizes the enduring nature of our identity in Christ in his book "In the Grip of Grace." He expresses it this way; "You have value simply because you exist—not because of what you do or have done—but purely because you are. "Lucado's words remind us that our value and sense of self are not dependent on our accomplishments or external situations. Instead, they originate from the truth that a higher power has lovingly and purposefully created us.

Understanding and embracing our identity in Christ can be an incredible source of motivation and encouragement. It verifies that we are never alone on our journeys because we have the guiding light of Christ illuminating our path. As Tim Keller, an author and theologian, expresses in his book "The Reason for

God ", "Jesus Christ doesn't merely provide comfort for maintaining the status quo; He challenges it." Keller's words remind us that fully embracing our identity in Christ might require us to step out of our comfort zones and embrace His transformative call to a life filled with His love.

Our identity in Christ gives us hope and resilience during times of hardship. The Apostle Paul beautifully captures this sentiment in his letter to the Corinthians: "But we have this treasure in jars of clay to show that this extraordinary power comes from God and not from ourselves. "Amid challenges, we find ourselves pressed from all sides but not crushed. We may need clarification. We never fall into despair. Though we may face persecution, we are never left alone. Even if circumstances strike us down, they cannot destroy us. These words from Paul remind us that our identity in Christ empowers us to overcome any obstacle that comes our way. In moments of weakness, it is through God's strength that we find perfection.

As we journey through the complexities of life, it is vital to remember the unchanging truth of who we are in Christ. Through the wisdom shared by Bible scholars and Christian authors, we are urged to embrace the fact that our worth and purpose go beyond worldly standards. They are rooted in the love and grace bestowed upon us by our saviour. Let us confidently walk in this truth and allow it to guide our steps while illuminating our path forward. By doing so, we will inspire others to follow suit and create a ripple effect of transformative change within the world around us.

Preserving our essence amidst the ever-changing world is like protecting a flickering flame amid a raging storm – it may seem challenging, but it's vital. This flame is our guiding light, illuminating our path and helping us navigate life's uncertainties.

To navigate the challenges of upholding our identity, we must deeply immerse ourselves in the wisdom found within God's Word.

In his letter, the apostle James advises us to not listen to the word but to put it into action, warning against self-deception (James 1:22). Charles Spurgeon, a known Christian author, adds to this thought by saying that a Bible falling apart is usually owned by someone who truly lives by it (Spurgeon, 1). These words serve as a reminder that our spiritual identities are not solely determined by what we know but rather by how God's Word actively transforms us.

Maintaining our identity amidst the ever-changing world is undeniably challenging yet absolutely necessary. Our understanding of God's nature, our willingness to surrender ourselves completely, our trust in His unwavering presence, and our immersion in His Word. May we find inspiration and guidance from these truths as we navigate through life's challenges and keep the flame of our spirituality burning bright.

Chapter Four

In His Kingdom Values

---◆O◆---

Living a Righteous Life in a World Filled with Turmoil

In a world engulfed in chaos and Darkness where moral decay seems to overshadow righteousness, there exists an enduring guidebook that illuminates Kingdom Values: This captivating book serves as a beacon of hope, urging us to navigate through the challenges of our fallen existence while upholding divine principles.

Esteemed men of faith and renowned scholars of the Bible, such as John C. Maxwell, in his work "The 21 Irrefutable Laws of Leadership ", affirm that living righteously entails aligning our actions with God's timeless standards. It is not about adhering to a set of regulations or religious rituals; instead, it is a conscious decision to embody love, integrity, Compassion and humility in every aspect of our lives.

Joyce Meyer, a Christian author and motivational speaker, emphasizes in her enlightening book "Battlefield of the Mind" that the battle for righteous living begins within us. By renewing our minds, we can overcome temptations and choose thoughts that honour God. Meyer asserts that embracing values enables us to tap into divine wisdom and experience true freedom and abundance by aligning our lives with His will.

Living a life of righteousness in a world filled with challenges is like climbing a hill. However, we embark on this journey with courage guided by the teachings of God's Word. This chapter titled "Kingdom Values; Living Righteously in a Fallen World" urges us to act and become the salt and light that our world desperately needs to see righteousness prevail. As the Apostle Paul wrote in his letter to the Philippians, "Focus your thoughts on things that are truly noble, right pure lovely admirable. Anything excellent or praiseworthy." (Philippians 4:8)

By embracing these Kingdom Values, we can rise above the Darkness. Inspire others to do the same. Together, we can leave a lasting impact on this fallen world. Let these profound principles guide you like a compass towards leading a purposeful life rooted in divine wisdom.

In our pursuit of embracing God's Kingdom. Where love triumphs over hate, Compassion over indifference, and goodness over evil. Lies the very essence of our purpose here on Earth. It is through our lives and tangible actions that we have the power to transform these intentional choices into visible manifestations of God's Kingdom right here, on Earth.

One practical step is to practice kindness and Compassion towards others. Matthew Henry, a known scholar of the Bible, reminds us that "compassion will guide us in the most effective ways to do good." When we approach others with love and empathy, we create an environment that nurtures respect and understanding. By listening to each other's stories and helping those in need, we can become beacons of hope and love in a world often clouded by Darkness.

Our commitment to righteousness and justice plays a role in upholding these values when faced with challenges. The biblical principle of Micah 6:8 encourages us to "act love mercy and walk humbly with your God." We are called upon to pursue justice for marginalized individuals, champion the voiceless, and work towards dismantling oppressive systems. This might involve engaging in protests, advocating for policy changes that promote equality, or supporting organizations dedicated to serving the underprivileged. Our actions must align with the values of the Kingdom we strive to foster.

In light of negativity and overwhelming Darkness, our faith must remain unwavering. Max Lucado, an author, reminds us that "faith is not merely believing that God will grant our every desire. "We hold the belief that God will always do what is right." During times, we can find solace in turning to God, knowing that His wisdom and guidance are constantly present. By engaging in prayer, meditation and studying God's teachings, we strengthen our determination to embody the values of His Kingdom and persevere when faced with opposition.

As we embark on this journey to embrace the Kingdom of God, let us not forget that real change happens through actions in our everyday lives. By showing kindness and Compassion, offering forgiveness, advocating for justice, and remaining steadfast in our faith, we have the power to make an impact on our world one intentional choice at a time. May each day begin with a renewed commitment to cultivate the Kingdom of God here on Earth and create a society rooted in love and justice.

Let us bring forth this Kingdom through choices and meaningful deeds.

In a world plagued by chaos and suffering, it is our decision to embrace the Kingdom of God that sets us apart. It is by displaying acts of love, Compassion and righteousness that we breathe life into this extraordinary Kingdom."

As N.T. Wright, a respected scholar of the Bible, wisely asserts, "The essence of the gospel goes beyond mere celebration and sacrifice; it encompasses a deep longing for a fair society, a longing that stems from the joy found in the Kingdom" (Wright, 120). The Kingdom of God is not an abstract idea but a tangible reality that compels us to act.

When we choose love over hatred, we rise above our human instincts and demonstrate maturity and wisdom. As C.S. Lewis eloquently puts it, "Don't waste time pondering whether you 'love' your neighbour; instead, act as if you do" (Lewis, 45). Love isn't merely an emotion; it's a choice to treat others with kindness, Compassion and acceptance. By embodying God's love within us, we become beacons of hope and illumination in this world that yearns for it desperately.

Compassion also plays a role in manifesting the Kingdom of God in our midst. As expressed profoundly by Henri Nouwen, an author, "Compassion impels us to venture into painful places; to embrace brokenness; to share in fear, confusion and anguish. "Compassion compels us to extend our empathy to those who are suffering to share in the sorrow of the lonely and to shed tears alongside those in pain (Nouwen, 82). When we consciously choose Compassion or indifference, we open ourselves up to the struggles of others and actively work towards alleviating their hardships. Compassion has the power to break down barriers and foster unity, understanding and love.

Moreover, when we make the choice for goodness over evil, we actively resist the forces of Darkness that exist in our world. As theologian Jonathan Edwards wisely stated, "The only genuine and sufficient motivation for any behaviour is the glorification of God" (Edwards, 56). Opting for goodness means aligning our desires with God's will and seeking His glory in everything we do. It means making choices that promote justice, fairness, integrity and righteousness. Ultimately, goodness prevails over evil; by embodying excellence ourselves, we contribute to establishing God's Kingdom on Earth.

We are called upon to embrace God's Kingdom by prioritizing love over hate, Compassion over indifference, and goodness over evil. Through choices and actions rooted in these principles, we breathe life into this Kingdom.

May this part of our journey serve as a source of motivation and empowerment, encouraging us to live out our faith in ways that can bring about positive transformations in our own lives as well as the lives of those around us.

Allow yourself to be moulded rather than conforming to worldly norms.

As we venture deeper into our core being, we often encounter a world filled with distractions posed by standards and earthly temptations. However, beneath these surface-level trappings lies our authentic selves waiting patiently to be discovered and embraced. It is through the stillness of the heart and surrendering our desires to God's guidance that our true selves begin to emerge.

Our true essence resides within our souls than in the external aspects of our existence. As we become more aware of our souls yearning for a connection with the divine, we embark on a journey to discover meaning and purpose in our lives.

To truly embrace who we are meant to be, it is essential to adopt the values of God's Kingdom as rooted in His teachings. Love is one value that the apostle Paul eloquently describes in 1 Corinthians 13:4-7. By embracing the love that mirrors God's love, we are able to transcend self-centeredness and cultivate Compassion and concern for others. When we embrace humility, our focus shifts from being self-centred to embodying a mindset of selflessness. We recognize that our worth lies in our relationship with God and serving His creation.

It is crucial to understand that the pursuit of discovering ourselves and our purpose should not be seen as separate from God's will. In fact, it is through aligning ourselves with His plan that we genuinely find our calling.

Discovering ourselves and our purpose through Kingdom values has a transformative effect. It helps us draw closer to God. Allows us to become vessels of His love and grace. Peter 2:9 tells us that we are chosen by God, a nation called out of Darkness into His marvellous light.

Let your inner compass guide you away.

These profound words resonate with our vision for living, reminding us that we are called to adhere to a moral standard. The fundamental approach to making choices and reaffirming Kingdom values lies within an awakened heart. We must strive for a comprehension of these spiritual virtues by studying God's teachings as proposed by N.T. Wright, an expert in Biblical scholarship. By immersing ourselves in Christ's teachings, we can discern the value of His Kingdom and strengthen our commitment to walking in His ways.

In our lives, we inevitably encounter numerous worldly temptations that threaten to divert our focus from Kingdom values. However, becoming disheartened by these enticements should serve as opportunities for personal growth and self-reflection.

Renowned biblical scholar John Piper highlights the importance of acknowledging our weaknesses. He emphasizes that when we recognize our vulnerabilities, we can find solace in God's refuge. Through His grace, God empowers us to overcome temptations and resist the allure of pleasures. This journey towards growth involves prayer, being accountable within a supportive community, and engaging in personal reflection.

To prioritize joy over fleeting gratification, we must shift our perspective and fix our gaze upon the everlasting. St. Augustine, a revered writer, explains that by understanding the transient nature of worldly pleasures, we can grasp the magnificence of eternal joy. It requires cultivating a mindset rooted in gratitude—recognizing that the delights offered by this world pale in comparison to the enduring blessings found within God's Kingdom. Regular contemplation of God's promises and reflecting on the inheritance awaiting us strengthens our determination to embrace Kingdom values.

Developing practices that enable us to stay focused on God's guiding light amid life's challenges is crucial. As suggested by Christian author Richard J. Foster, embracing disciplines such as solitude, meditation, and fasting helps remove distractions from our lives while aligning our hearts with God's voice.

Moreover, developing devotion and appreciation, actively participating in acts of kindness and seeking divine guidance through personal and communal prayer can strengthen our bond with the ultimate source of happiness and steer us away from life's temptations.

Adopting the principles of the Kingdom as our guiding principles necessitates action, yet the benefits are incalculable. By choosing and reaffirming these principles, we unlock access to everlasting joy and discover our purpose in this world.

Kingdom values speak softly. Humility and service.

Amidst a world dominated by the noise of priorities and self-centred values, a profound statement emerges: Kingdom values speak softly. Humility and service. These words hold truth, urging us to examine our lives and how we respond to the chaotic clamour surrounding us. How can we truly grasp these whispers of humility and service amidst the noise? How can we actively listen to them? Act upon their quiet yet powerful call? And, importantly, how can we embody and share these values to inspire others?

To truly hear the whispers of humility and service, one must nurture a receptive heart. Recognizing that the world often amplifies self-centred values, it becomes crucial to step away from distractions and find moments of solitude for reflection. In these moments, we can find inner peace and align ourselves with the gentle echoes of the Kingdom.

The whispers of the Kingdom become apparent when we immerse ourselves in acts of service. By seeking opportunities to serve others, we embody humility, Compassion and love towards our fellow human beings.

This could involve offering your time and assistance at a church and community, reaching out to those who are marginalized, or simply listening compassionately to those who are in need.

The apostle Paul, known for his humility and servanthood, understood the importance of helping others. In his writings, he said, "For even the Son of Man did not come to be served but to serve and give his life as a ransom for many" (Mark 10:45, NIV). By following the example of Christ, we go beyond our needs and embrace a life of selflessness.

Demonstrating Kingdom values through our actions has the power to bring about transformation. People are naturally drawn to authenticity and sincerity. When they see humility and service exemplified in their lives, they are inspired to follow suit. Our actions have the potential to influence others' perspectives and behaviours.

In a world that often celebrates selfishness and materialistic pursuits, it is vital for us to intentionally align our hearts with the callings of humility and service that stem from the Kingdom. By finding moments of silence amidst the noise, engaging in acts of kindness, and being role models for these values, we become catalysts for change in a world hungry for godly wisdom and authenticity.

Let us respond to the call and embrace the whispers of the Kingdom, allowing them to shape our lives and inspire others to embark on this extraordinary journey of adopting humility, service, and ultimately finding true peace and joy.

Plant seeds of Kingdom values in the soil of everyday life, and you will harvest a rich energy filled with joy, peace and righteousness. This profound wisdom, rooted in principles, encourages us to live a life that aligns with God's purposes, as N.T. Wright, a Bible scholar, states, "The Kingdom of God is not some distant dream but a reality that awaits our embrace in our day-to-day choices" (Wright, 2010, p. 87). Echoing this sentiment is Christian author John Piper, who says, "When we prioritize God's values in our actions and attitudes, we experience the fullness of life He desires for us" (Piper, 2003, p. 112). By nurturing a heart that seeks to honour God in all aspects of our lives, we can witness transformation not only in ourselves but also in those around us. Let us accept this invitation to sow Kingdom values with confidence that the harvest will be bountiful and overflowing with blessings from God.

Ray of hope and stability

In a world filled with turmoil, chaos and uncertainty, the concept of embracing and embodying Kingdom values in our lives offers a ray of hope and stability. It encourages us to embark on a journey where we intentionally sow seeds of love, kindness and Compassion, nurturing them as they flourish and bear fruit. Through this cultivation, not only do we reap the rewards of joy, peace and righteousness for ourselves, but we also enrich the lives of those around us.

To sow Kingdom values effectively, we must establish a connection with our Heavenly Father through prayer. By seeking God's guidance, strength and wisdom in our daily lives, our hearts align with His purposes. This alignment allows the Holy Spirit to transform our thoughts and actions so that they reflect God's desired values for His Kingdom.

Jesus taught us to love others just as He loved us—a commandment that lies at the core of Kingdom values. By seeking opportunities to demonstrate genuine love and kindness towards others, we plant seeds that have the power to bring about life-changing transformations.

By engaging in actions, we have the power to plant seeds that will grow into happiness, serenity and moral uprightness for ourselves and those in our vicinity.

The words we choose possess influence in lifting spirits, igniting inspiration, and bringing about restoration. When we speak truth with kindness and elegance, we sow seeds of authenticity and honesty. Nurturing a spirit of forgiveness enables us to sow seeds of reconciliation and renewal, creating an environment that aligns with values cherished by the Kingdom.

The Bible serves as a guiding beacon on our path towards sowing these Kingdom values. By devoting time to studying and contemplating God's Word, we equip ourselves with the tools to nurture growth and bear abundant fruits.

Indeed, sow Kingdom values require adopting a servant-like attitude. By emulating Christ's humility, we plant seeds of humility that lead to healing, reconciliation and unity. Renowned Christian author C.S. Lewis reminds us that humility is not about having an opinion of ourselves but rather placing less focus on our own needs. Cultivating humility allows us to prioritize the well-being of others over our desires while promoting joy, peace and righteousness in our interactions and relationships.

As we navigate through the ground of everyday life, sowing Kingdom values is not merely an idle endeavour but an intentional way of living.

Through the practice of heartfelt prayer, intentional love, speaking truth, studying Scripture and cultivating humility, we can witness the beautiful growth and flourishing of joy, peace and righteousness. Let us wholeheartedly embrace this transformative journey, ensuring that not only do we reap a bountiful harvest for ourselves but also enrich the lives of those around us.

Every step on the path of righteousness leaves lasting imprints.

The Bible, a scripture that serves as a guiding light in our lives, is filled with verses that illuminate the righteous path. As we embark on this soul-stirring journey, let us first turn to the words of the apostle Paul. In his letter to the Romans (Romans 14:17), he beautifully states that true godliness goes beyond physical needs and dwells in righteousness, peace and everlasting joy through the Holy Spirit. These profound words remind us that pursuing holiness nourishes our souls with happiness beyond earthly pleasures.

Drawing from the well of wisdom found within scriptures teachings, C.S. Lewis—an esteemed Christian author—shares transformative insights in his influential work "Mere Christianity." His words fortify our understanding of how each step taken on the path holds immense significance.

He explains that witnessing a man being taken to prison is akin to seeing a man undergoing a process towards becoming saintly (Lewis, 1952, p. 106). This powerful metaphor employed by Lewis highlights the idea that amidst worldly hardships, those who follow the path of righteousness are moulded into vessels of sanctity. Each challenge. Every difficulty endured becomes an opportunity for spiritual refinement.

The devout individuals, driven by their commitment to God's teachings, possess an unshakable faith that guides them through the storms of life. In the Gospel of Matthew, Jesus, who embodies love and Compassion, assures us of this eternal truth by stating, "I am the way and the truth and the life. No one comes to the father except, through me" (Matthew 14:6). These words serve as a reminder that by emulating Christ's example, we draw nearer to God. As we walk in His footsteps, we cast aside illusions that hinder our spiritual growth and discover a profound sense of purpose.

As we ponder these words, it becomes clear that walking in righteous ways leaves a lasting impact on our lives. By aligning our hearts with God's truth and following in the footsteps of those who have lived righteously before us, we unlock the potential within ourselves to rise above worldly illusions and draw nearer to God's heart. Let us, therefore, strive to journey on the path of righteousness while embracing the enduring imprints that guide us towards a life enriched by God's wisdom, love and blessings.

The mightiest oak stands tall and strong because it has weathered storms.

Upholding values in a world tainted by sin is undoubtedly a challenging voyage, one that necessitates unwavering faithfulness, resilience and perseverance. As we journey through life, we come across challenges and difficult situations that test our determination and weaken our dedication to the principles and values established by God. It is during these trying times, when we confront these challenges head-on while keeping our faith in God, that we discover the strength to remain steadfast and resolute like a mighty oak tree. This powerful imagery serves as a reminder that obstacles, although daunting, can actually be opportunities for growth and the revelation of our true character. By upholding the values of the Kingdom, we not only inspire and uplift others but also become shining beacons of hope and godly wisdom in a world filled with Darkness.

The Bible, which serves as the source of divine wisdom, provides us with numerous examples of individuals who remained faithful to God's values despite facing overwhelming adversity. One such example can be found in the book of Daniel. When Daniel and his three companions were taken captive and brought to Babylon, they were confronted with the challenge of staying true to their faith amidst a corrupt culture steeped in idolatry. Nevertheless, they stood firm in their commitment to obeying God's commands by refusing to partake in the food and wine from the King's table (Daniel 1:8). Their unwavering belief and trust in the faithfulness of God not only preserved their integrity but also positioned them for divine blessings and progress.

According to the Christian author and scholar A.W. Tozer, it's unfortunate that we often limit our plans to what we think we can accomplish on our own. He emphasized that God seeks individuals who are willing to be vessels for His extraordinary works. This insightful statement reminds us that in order to uphold the values of God's Kingdom, we must rely entirely on His strength and guidance. It is not through our abilities or human endeavours that we can navigate life's challenges and remain steadfast; instead, it is by surrendering ourselves to God's will and allowing Him to work through us. The Apostle Paul echoes this truth when he declares, "I am capable of achieving anything through Christ who empowers me" (Philippians 4:13).

As we embark on this demanding journey of upholding the principles of God's Kingdom, it is crucial to remember that we are not alone. We have been blessed with the Holy Spirit as a source of comfort, counsel and direction. C.S. Lewis reiterates this point in his book "Mere Christianity ", highlighting that true happiness and peace cannot exist apart from God Himself because they are intrinsically connected.

Genuine contentment, happiness and tranquillity can only be discovered when we find solace in God and align our lives with His purposes and principles. It is during these times that we truly learn to depend on God, placing our trust in Him to grant us the fortitude and bravery required to stay committed to the values of His Kingdom.

Upholding the values of God's Kingdom in a world tainted by sin is undeniably a journey. Nonetheless, as long as we keep our focus on God and place our confidence in His unwavering faithfulness, we can stand tall and resolute like a mighty oak tree amidst life's storms. As we navigate through these tempests, may we draw inspiration and encouragement from characters like Daniel and his companions. Let us also remember the words of A.W. Tozer and C.S. Lewis that remind us of the imperative nature of relying on God's strength and abiding in His presence. Upholding the values of God's Kingdom may not be a task. Still, it is a noble pursuit that has the potential to inspire and transform lives within this fallen world.

The principles of God's Kingdom serve as a guiding force, helping us turn challenges into pathways that lead us to ourselves in Christ. These words capture the impact of embracing the values of God's Kingdom. In a world filled with uncertainty, difficulties and trials, the principles rooted in God's Kingdom can. Steer us towards becoming our most authentic and most fulfilled selves in Christ.

One remarkable aspect of the journey is how it interprets challenges as opportunities for personal growth and progress. This perspective is beautifully expressed by N.T Wright, a Bible scholar, in his book "Surprised by Hope." Wright reminds us that resurrection encompasses not only life after death but also life before death. He encourages us to view the obstacles we face through the lens of kingdom values. Allowing challenges to discourage us, we are encouraged to perceive them as bridges that can lead us towards a deeper connection with Christ and the realization of our full potential as His followers.

The foundation for this transformative process lies in embodying kingdom values in our lives.

In his book titled "Sermon on the Mount ", Dietrich Bonhoeffer emphasizes that followers of Jesus should prioritize their relationship with God over worldly concerns. This implies that we should not dwell on the difficulties we encounter but focus on nurturing our connection with God; we cultivate a resilient spirit that enables us to confront challenges head-on, relying on God's strength and wisdom to guide us.

The profound impact of embracing kingdom values is genuinely remarkable. C.S. Lewis beautifully captures this idea in his work "Mere Christianity," stating, "It is when I turn to Christ that I discover what I truly seek." When we wholeheartedly commit ourselves to following Christ and incorporating his teachings as the guiding principles in our lives, we undergo a transformation. Our character is refined, our perspectives. Our actions are driven by love, mercy and Compassion. This transformative process not only benefits us individually but also has a ripple effect on the world around us.

Martin Luther King Jr., a reformer, exemplifies the power of embracing Kingdom values even in the face of immense challenges. In the book titled "Strength to Love ", the author expresses a message; "Darkness cannot overcome Darkness; only light has that ability. Hate cannot conquer hate; only love can do so." The unwavering dedication of King towards justice, equality and love not only influenced the civil rights movement in America but also touched the hearts of those who encountered his words. His life stands as a testament to the impact that embracing values rooted in kindness and Compassion can have on our world, inspiring us to follow suit.

When we wholeheartedly embrace these values, we realize that challenges no longer hinder our progress but instead present opportunities for growth, learning and transformation.

Transforming challenges into bridges that lead us closer to becoming ourselves in Christ embodies a profound truth.

By embracing the principles of God's Kingdom, we develop a perspective on life that allows us to see challenges as opportunities for personal growth. This outlook also inspires others to do the same. Drawing wisdom from Bible scholars, Christian authors and the examples of those who have come before us, we can fully embrace the values of God's Kingdom and unlock our true potential as followers of Christ. Let us all find encouragement in embarking on this journey of transformation, knowing that God's guidance will lead us to become the versions of ourselves through Christ.

Bring light to Darkness and wounds and spark waves of change.

The values of God's Kingdom bring light to Darkness and wounds and ignite powerful waves of change. These impactful words capture the influence that comes with embracing these values. In a world filled with Darkness, brokenness and despair, the principles found within God's Kingdom hold the potential to bring illumination, healing and transformation. As N.T. Wright beautifully articulates in his book "Christian" "The kingdom of God is focused on healing our world rather than abandoning it." When we align our lives with these values, we become catalysts for change—offering hope, restoration and love to those around us.

The concept of bringing light to Darkness holds importance in the teachings of Jesus. In the Gospel of John, John expresses this idea by saying, "In him was life and that life was the light of all mankind. The light shines in the darkness. The darkness has not overcome it" (John 1:4-5 NIV). This reminds us that when we embrace God's kingdom values, we become carriers of His light radiating brightly in challenging times. Our words, actions and attitudes can dispel ignorance, offer understanding and reveal the truth.

Another transformative aspect emphasized by kingdom values is healing wounds. The known Christian author Henri Nouwen beautifully captures this idea in his book titled "The Wounded Healer," where he states that nobody escapes experiencing injuries in their lives – whether physical, emotional, mental or spiritual. The crucial question then becomes not how we can hide our wounds but how we can utilize our own woundedness to serve others. When we fully embrace God's kingdom values, it is our calling to extend Compassion, empathy and healing to those who are suffering.

When we offer love and understanding, we become vehicles for the healing grace of God, bringing restoration and wholeness to those who are hurting.

Embracing the values of the Kingdom naturally leads to sparking waves of change. In his letter to the Romans, the apostle Paul advises us not to conform to the ways of this world but instead to be transformed by renewing our minds (Romans 12:2 NIV). When we align our thoughts, beliefs and actions with God's kingdom values, we become catalysts for transformation within our communities and beyond. C.S. Lewis eloquently captures this idea in his book "The Weight of Glory ", expressing that it is significant to remember that even the ordinary individuals we encounter could one day become beings worthy of worship. By embodying these kingdom values, we inspire others to embrace their potential and contribute towards transforming the world around them.

These values can significantly influence our lives and the world. We are reminded that when we align ourselves with these principles, we become catalysts for brightness, restoration and positive growth. As we embark on this journey, let us be motivated to bring hope, love and constructive transformation to those around us. It is through God's Kingdom values that even the darkest corners can be illuminated; the deepest wounds can be waves of change that can be set in motion.

Chapter Five
In His Kingdom Wisdom

---◆○◆---

Seeking God's Guidance in Decision-making

Have you ever found yourself longing for guidance in the midst of life's choices? If so, I invite you to explore the pages of "Kingdom Wisdom; Seeking God's Guidance in Decision Making." This remarkable book takes you on a journey equipping you with deep insight and understanding to navigate life's critical turning points.

At the core of this captivating story lies a truth: seeking God's guidance is not just a religious ritual but an opportunity to cultivate a personal and profound connection with the Divine. Esteemed scholars and respected authors within the community have beautifully expressed that pursuing Kingdom wisdom is not limited to moments of crisis or significant decisions; it is an ongoing thread woven into every aspect of our lives.

Christian writer and leadership expert John Maxwell emphasizes in his influential work "Today Matters," that our choices hold immense power in shaping both the direction and destiny of our lives. This profound realization serves as a reminder that seemingly minor decisions possess the potential to shape our experiences and influence those around us.

When we begin to understand the significance of our choices, we realize the urgency of seeking guidance from a power. We recognize that only God can truly comprehend the reaching impact our decisions can have.

In our exploration of "Kingdom Wisdom ", we will dive into the teachings of scripture, drawing insights from Bible scholars like Henry Cloud and John Townsend. Their renowned work, "Boundaries ", emphasizes the importance of aligning our decision-making process with God's principles. They remind us that wisdom is not detached from our lives but intricately woven into every aspect of our thoughts, words and actions. By establishing boundaries, we protect our hearts and minds while allowing God's wisdom to flow freely. This transformation leads us to make purpose-driven decisions of self-serving ones.

As we embark on this inspiring journey, we will also encounter timeless wisdom from Proverbs, referred to as the book of practical knowledge. Proverbs 3:5-6 guides us to "trust in the Lord with all your heart and lean not on your understanding. These enduring words resonate an invitation from above—to surrender our human knowledge and place unwavering trust in the boundless wisdom of our Heavenly Father.

Throughout the stories in the Bible, we can find examples of individuals who sought God's guidance when faced with important decisions. One notable instance is when King Solomon became king and recognized his need for wisdom to rule effectively (1 Kings 3 9). This serves as a lesson for us, showing that seeking wisdom from God is crucial in our own pursuit of understanding His Kingdom. Additionally, the apostle James encourages believers to approach God, knowing that He generously grants wisdom to those who ask (James 1:5).

Kingdom Wisdom not only provides theological foundations for seeking God's guidance but also offers practical tools for discernment. Inspired by Christian mentors like Charles Stanley and Joyce Meyer, it challenges us to develop a lifestyle centred on prayer, meditation and intentional listening. By dedicating time to connect with our Heavenly Father, we become more attuned to His gentle voice amid the noise of daily distractions.

Seeking God's Guidance in Decision Making serves as a testament to the transformative impact of aligning our choices with divine wisdom.

By drawing from the wisdom of Bible scholars and Christian authors, this narrative enriches our spirits, ignites our passion and empowers us to make choices that honour God and bring blessings to those around us. Together, let's embark on this journey as we embrace a life guided by kingdom wisdom that surpasses our understanding and propels us into boundless possibilities rooted in the heart of our Heavenly Father.

Silence is like soil where divine guidance blossoms.

In the realm of wisdom, silence holds more meaning than just the absence of noise; it signifies a state of deep receptiveness. It is within the tranquillity of our hearts that divine guidance finds ground to manifest itself and flourish. As we immerse ourselves in the embrace of silence, we open ourselves up to a realm beyond comprehension, where God's whispers gently lead us towards making sound decisions.

The pursuit of wisdom requires more than knowledge; it calls for a humble heart and attentive ears. The apostle James reminds us to "be quick to listen slow to speak" (James 1;19). In a world filled with noise and distractions, it becomes increasingly challenging to discern the voice of wisdom. However, if we are willing to cultivate an attitude of silence, we invite counsel into every aspect of our lives.

To seek guidance from God, we must consciously choose to distance ourselves from the chaos of the world and enter into a state of silence. It is in this practice of silence that we open up room for God to communicate with us, like how the prophet Elijah heard God's voice in a gentle whisper after the wind, earthquake and fire (1 Kings 19;11 12). We, too, can listen to His gentle stories when we calm our minds.

Renowned Christian author Richard J. Foster highlights the impact of silence in his book "Celebration of Discipline; The Path to Spiritual Growth." He explains that if solitude is like an examination room for our souls, then silence acts as an MRI scanner. In moments of silence, our spirits are revealed in ways that self-centeredness often obscures (Foster, 1988, p. 101). Foster encourages us to let go of the distractions brought on by our egos and embrace the clarity and discernment that silence provides as we seek God's guidance.

Embracing silence is embarking on a journey within ourselves. By relinquishing our agendas and desires, we create a space within us where God's wisdom can thrive and grow.

In her book titled "Listening to God: Cultivating a Conversational Connection with the Divine ", author Joyce Huggett emphasizes the impact of silence on our personal growth. She suggests that silence not only allows us to interpret our experiences but also leads us towards their transformation (Huggett, 1993, p. 8). Through moments of stillness, we not only learn to listen attentively but also embrace obedience to the gentle whispers of the divine, guiding us towards making wise choices.

The wisdom expressed in the Bible beautifully encapsulates the essence of seeking God's guidance through contemplation. The Psalmist encourages us with the words, "Be calm and acknowledge that I am God" (Psalm 46;10 NIV). This timeless invitation reminds us that when we find solace in silence, we encounter the presence of a power. In our hearts, we become attuned to discerning His guiding whispers.

As we navigate through life's journey seeking wisdom and enlightenment, we must maintain discipline in cultivating moments of silence and attentive listening. Christian writer Henri Nouwen wisely advises us that embarking on a path requires courage – specifically entering into the desert-like solitude within ourselves – so that through gentle and persistent efforts, it may transform into a vibrant garden filled with privacy (Nouwen, 1972 p.19). It is within this wilderness of confidentiality that we discover whispers blooming into profound revelations from God.

In conclusion, the pursuit of wisdom encourages us to value moments of silence. By creating space for silence in our lives, we invite the blossoming of guidance within us. Let us pay attention to the teachings of Bible scholars and Christian authors who have shed light on this path for us. In the peacefulness of silence, we discover the insight needed to make choices and embark on a purposeful and satisfying journey in God's presence.

To truly grasp God's wisdom, one must embrace His timing when answers are revealed. In a world that prioritizes gratification and quick solutions, we often find ourselves impatiently searching for answers to our prayers and seeking clarity in decision-making. However, genuine wisdom comes from trusting God's timeline rather than relying solely on our own sense of urgency. It is during moments of waiting and throughout the journey that our faith is tested and refined. It is through God's time that His purpose and plan for our lives become evident.

The idea of embracing God's timing stems from the biblical belief that all things work according to His purpose and will.

The apostle Paul reminds us in Romans 8:28, "We are aware that God works for the benefit of those who love Him and have been called according to His purpose" (NIV). This verse provides reassurance that when faced with uncertainty and unanswered prayers, God is actively working behind the scenes, orchestrating events in His perfect timing for our ultimate well-being.

Throughout the Bible, we encounter instances where individuals had to patiently wait for God's timing. Joseph endured years of hardships and betrayals before becoming second in command to the Pharaoh of Egypt. Similarly, Abraham and Sarah had to trust in God's promise of having a child despite it seeming impossible due to their age. These stories teach us the significance of surrendering our timelines and putting our trust in God's wisdom and providence.

Christian author and speaker Iyanla Vanzant encourages readers in her book "In the Meantime; Finding Yourself and the Love You Want" to embrace God's timing. She writes, "God has a plan, for your life. Have faith that every moment unfolds exactly as it should regardless of its appearance or feeling" (Vanzant, 54).

Vanzant's words serve as a reminder that when faced with uncertainty and waiting, we can take solace in the knowledge that God is in control.

C.S. Lewis, a Christian writer, echoes a similar sentiment in his book "Mere Christianity." He beautifully expresses how humans are both physical beings, existing within the constraints of time while belonging to an eternal world (Lewis, 78). This delicate balance highlights the importance of placing our trust in God's timing and recognizing that His ways surpass our own.

Trusting in God's timing doesn't mean adopting an approach to decision-making. On the contrary, it encourages us to seek His guidance and attentively listen for His voice in our lives. John Ortberg, an author and pastor, emphasizes this point in his book "The Life You've Always Wanted," highlighting that discernment involves distinguishing between what is genuinely right versus what is only partially correct (Ortberg, 112).

When we let go of our plans and seek divine guidance, we gain the ability to recognize the perfect timing of God and make choices that align with His desires.

In summary, comprehending God's wisdom necessitates embracing His timing as He reveals answers. It is by relying on His clock rather than our alarms that we uncover His purpose and blueprint for our lives. As believers, we can find solace in knowing that God orchestrates all things for our benefit and that His ways surpass ours. During times of waiting and throughout our journey, we develop trust in His wisdom. Actively seek His direction when making decisions. By embracing God's flawless timing, we are able to discover inspiration, encouragement and the richness of knowledge.

God illuminates our steps while not constantly unveiling the map.

Have you ever experienced a sense of being lost or uncertain about where your path was leading? Have you ever examined your crafted map only to realize that it failed to light up the way forward? In those moments of doubt, it is crucial to remember that God guides us step by step rather than revealing the whole map. He serves as our guiding light, leading us on a captivating journey filled with faith and self-discovery.

As followers of the faith, we are called to place our trust in the divine guidance of God, understanding that every step we take with unwavering faith will reveal the path that lies ahead.

In the scriptures, specifically in Psalm 119, 105, it is stated, "Your word serves as a guiding light for my journey and illuminates my path." This profound verse reminds us that God's Word encompasses more than stories or moral lessons; it serves as a brilliant source of wisdom and direction. When we wholeheartedly immerse ourselves in His teachings, we discover that they illuminate our way forward, offering us clarity and purpose. Just as a lamp exudes brightness amidst darkness, too does God's Word provide us with hope and assurance during times of uncertainty.

Placing our trust in God's guidance necessitates taking a leap of faith and surrendering our plans and desires. Letting go of the perceived control we have over our lives may present challenges; however, doing so opens up doors to possibilities that lie ahead. Proverbs 3 5 6 offers encouragement by stating, "Trust, in the LORD do not rely solely on your own understanding. In all your ways acknowledge Him. He will make your paths straight."When we place our trust in God and surrender our actions to Him, He will pave the way for us to remove obstacles and guide us towards our ultimate destination.

The path of faith is only sometimes straightforward or easily discernible. There may be moments when we're unable to perceive what lies beyond the next step. However, it is in these instances of uncertainty that our faith is truly tested and strengthened. The book of Hebrews 11:1 reminds us that "faith is being sure of what we hope for and certain of what we do not see." Our belief in God's guidance should remain steadfast even when the road ahead appears dim or unfamiliar. Instead, we are called to take a leap of faith, confident that God will illuminate our journey one step at a time.

As we proceed with each step in faith, we begin to uncover the beauty in the journey itself. It is simple to become fixated on reaching the destination, constantly striving for a significant milestone or accomplishment. However, authentic joy can be found within the process – within the growth and transformation that transpire along the way. As stated by Apostle Paul in Philippians 3:14, "I press on toward the goal to win the prize for which God has called me heavenward in Christ Jesus. "Paul recognized that the process of reaching a goal holds value just as much as achieving the plan itself. With every step taken in faith, he discovered more of God's grace and the path that had been prepared.

In conclusion, my friends, let us always bear in mind that it is God who guides our individual journeys. Though our map may not always be clear, we can trust in His guidance. His Word serves as a guiding light illuminating our path. Let us surrender our plans to Him, for He will direct us towards ways. Have unwavering faith in things not yet seen because faith is the assurance of things hoped for. As you embark on your journey, remember that each step taken in faith reveals the pathway ahead and brings you closer to the ultimate reward – eternal life with our Heavenly Father. May God bless you abundantly throughout your journey guided by faith.

The wisdom of God shapes our decisions, transforming them into blueprints that manifest in our lives. When it comes to mapping out our journey, there is no source of guidance and inspiration other than seeking the wisdom of our Heavenly Father. It is through His knowledge that we discover direction, purpose and a blueprint for a fulfilling and significant existence. Throughout history, esteemed scholars of the Bible and authors grounded in Christianity have stressed the significance of seeking God's guidance. Their profound insights offer wisdom and encouragement.

The book of Proverbs, renowned as a reservoir of wisdom within the Bible, provides guidance for navigating life's intricacies. Solomon, recognized as the individual to have ever lived, declares in Proverbs 3:5-6, "Trust in the Lord with all your heart and do not rely on your own understanding; in all your ways submit to him, and he will make your paths straight." This poignant verse serves as a reminder to surrender our plans and desires to God while entrusting His wisdom to lead us on the right course.

In the book "Knowing God " written by the renowned Bible scholar J.I. Packer, he emphasizes the importance of seeking God's guidance. According to Packer, what truly matters in the end is not our knowledge of God but the more profound truth that He knows us intimately. This serves as a reminder that seeking God's guidance goes beyond finding answers; it involves surrendering ourselves to His wisdom and allowing Him to shape our lives according to His divine plan.

John Eldredge, a respected Christian author, explores the transformative power of seeking God's wisdom in his book "Walking with God." Eldredge highlights that every path designed by God is filled with love and consideration for us. He assures us that nothing good for us will be withheld from us. This reminds us that when we seek His guidance, we can trust that every path He leads us on is, ultimately, for our benefit.

Additionally, in his epistle, the Apostle James encourages believers to seek God's wisdom when making decisions. In the verses James 1 5 6, it is stated that if any of us lack knowledge, we should turn to God, who generously grants wisdom to everyone without finding fault. He assures us that if we ask with faith and without doubt, He will provide us with the knowledge we seek. James emphasizes the significance of having faith and trust in God's wisdom. By seeking His guidance, not only do we acquire knowledge but also strengthen our relationship with Him.

Corrie ten Boom shares her testimony in her influential book called "The Hiding Place." She recounts how she sought God's guidance during the most challenging circumstances. According to her words of giving instructions to God, we should simply report for duty. This quote serves as a reminder that seeking God's guidance does not involve dictating what He should do but humbly submitting ourselves to Him and aligning our hearts with His divine will.

When we seek God's guidance, His wisdom shapes our decisions like blueprints that manifest in our lives. Bible scholars and Christian authors alike encourage us to trust in Him, relinquish our own understanding and submit ourselves to His divine plan.

As we navigate through the complexities of life, let us remember the words of Solomon, J.I. Packer, John Eldredge, Apostle James and Corrie ten Boom. They all remind us to seek God's wisdom as we plan our paths. May their teachings inspire us to depend on God's loving guidance and find purpose, fulfilment and a life that reflects His plan. Let us actively seek His wisdom because it is through Him that we discover lasting satisfaction.

God's guidance always leads upward rather than just pointing in a specific direction.

When faced with the crossroads of life, use the compass of Kingdom wisdom to guide you. God's guidance always leads upward rather than just pointing north or south. In this changing and uncertain world, it is crucial to have a trustworthy source of direction and wisdom. The compass of Kingdom wisdom is rooted in God's Word. Provides a guiding light that goes beyond earthly navigation. This wisdom brings inspiration, encouragement and godly insights that empower individuals to make choices even in challenging circumstances. As respected Bible scholars and Christian authors confirm, delving into the depths of God's guidance leads to a journey that navigates life's crossroads towards spiritual growth, purposefulness and fulfilment.

The idea of Kingdom wisdom is deeply rooted in the Scriptures. In the book of Proverbs, King Solomon, known for his wisdom, wrote, "Place your trust in the Lord and don't rely solely on your own understanding. In all aspects of life surrender to Him. He will guide you along the right path" (Proverbs 3;5 6 NIV). The compass of Kingdom wisdom involves recognizing that our own understanding is limited and submitting to God's guidance. By acknowledging our dependence on Him, we open ourselves to a perspective that surpasses the constraints of our human minds.

Warren W. Wiersbe, a scholar of biblical texts, explains the upward nature of God's guidance in his book titled "Be Skilful; God's Guidebook to Wise Living." He emphasizes that God doesn't promise to guide us towards directions like north or south or east or west; instead, His guidance leads us upward. This distinction is crucial as it highlights how God's guidance transcends orientations and directs us towards spiritual growth by aligning our lives with His purposes and His Kingdom.

Navigating through moments in life often entails making challenging decisions. To make choices during these times, we require inspiration and encouragement, which Kingdom wisdom offers.

In his book titled "The Purpose Driven Life ", Rick Warren shares the idea that when we encounter detours in our lives, it is because God intends to shape and strengthen our character (Warren, 2002). This perspective reminds us that when faced with unexpected twists and turns, God's guidance is at work, moulding us into individuals who mirror His character.

John Eldredge, another author, echoes this viewpoint in his book called "Walking with God: Talk to Him. Hear from Him. Really." He writes about how the primary purpose of God is to guide us towards becoming the person we are meant to be by leading us through genuine repentance (Eldredge, 2009). Embracing God's guidance at a crossroads in life entails surrendering our own desires and aligning ourselves with His plans. It is through this process of repentance and transformation that we discover purpose and fulfilment.

The compass of Kingdom wisdom not only directs us towards higher ideals but also empowers us to discern the right path among a multitude of choices. Charles R. Swindoll, another Christian author, offers an insightful perspective in his book titled "Living Above the Level of Mediocrity: A Commitment to Excellence."He states, "Wisdom is a gift from God that enables us to perceive life with exceptional objectivity and manage it with exceptional stability" (Swindoll, 2006). This wisdom empowers us to make choices that align with God's desires and reflect His nature in uncertain circumstances.

Embarking on the journey of life's moments with the guidance of Kingdom wisdom is both inspiring and transformative. As affirmed by scholars of the Bible and authors within the Christian community, God's guidance extends beyond mere cardinal directions. By trusting in the Lord and submitting to His leading, we can discover growth, purpose and fulfilment. Embracing turns in our path while making wise decisions amidst challenges fosters personal growth. It brings us closer to God's plan. Additionally, Kingdom wisdom equips us with the ability to discern the course of action and navigate life with remarkable objectivity and stability. Thus, let us anchor our lives in the wisdom found within God's Word—a source of empowerment that helps us navigate life's crossroads while experiencing divine transformation.

Flourish in your destined field just as a sunflower does.

"Like sunflowers are drawn towards sunlight may your decisions be guided by Gods wisdom. Flourish, in your destined field just as a sunflower does."

Sunflowers are well known for their ability to turn towards the sun and follow its path across the sky. This captivating phenomenon can inspire us to align our choices and actions with the wisdom of power. Similar to how sunflowers bloom in their designated fields, we, too, can. Fulfil our purpose when we seek guidance from a higher source and follow its lead.

The importance of seeking wisdom and guidance can be found throughout various passages in the Bible. In Proverbs 3:5-6 an esteemed biblical scholar named Solomon reminds us, "Place your trust in the LORD do not rely solely on your own understanding; acknowledge him in all your ways, and he will make your paths straight." This verse emphasizes the necessity of surrendering our limited understanding and placing our trust in the wisdom of a higher power. By doing we receive assurance that we will be guided along straight paths. This assurance should serve as encouragement for us to rely on wisdom rather than solely relying on our own imperfect perception.

In his book titled "Mere Christianity ", C.S. Lewis, a Christian author, highlights the significance of aligning our decisions with divine wisdom. He explains that "mere improvement" is not equivalent to redemption; however, rescue always leads to improvement within this present moment. Ultimately, it will elevate individuals beyond what they can envision.

In his writings, Lewis emphasizes how God's wisdom can bring about transformations in our lives. When we make decisions based on His guidance, not only do we experience personal growth, but we also draw closer to our ultimate redemption. This insight serves as a reminder that seeking God's wisdom is more than just self-improvement; it is an integral part of our spiritual journey.

In his book "The Purpose Driven Life ", Christian author Rick Warren underscores the significance of flourishing in the area where God has placed us. He expresses, "You were created by God and for God, and until you grasp that truth, life will never truly make sense." Warren reminds us that our purpose is intricately tied to God's plan for us. By aligning our choices with His wisdom, we thrive in the domain where He has positioned us. This understanding infuses our lives with meaning and purpose.

Drawing inspiration from the analogy of a sunflower, Bible scholar Timothy Keller urges us to seek God's wisdom in all aspects of our existence. In his work

"The Reason for God ", Keller asserts, "We must recognize that at our best moments, love and faithfulness can fall short; yet in our worst moments, God loves and remains steadfast."" of seeking permission, we should seek God's guidance. Aligning our decisions with wisdom is the key to unlocking our divine potential." These profound words encapsulate a shift in how we approach the choices and challenges that life presents to us. In a world that often prioritizes logic and societal standards, this call to seek guidance from God directs our attention towards the timeless. It taps into a wellspring of wisdom and strength beyond our own capabilities. By drawing inspiration from Bible scholars and Christian authors, we delve deeper into this narrative, discovering the profound impact of aligning our choices with heavenly wisdom.

The Bible serves as the source of divine guidance, showcasing numerous instances where seeking God's wisdom led to remarkable breakthroughs and empowered individuals to fulfil their true potential. In the book of Proverbs, King Solomon, known for his wisdom, imparts this enduring truth; "Place your trust in the Lord and do not rely solely on your own understanding. In all aspects of life surrender to Him. He will guide you on straight paths" (Proverbs 3;5 6 NIV). This verse highlights the importance of acknowledging our limited understanding while submitting ourselves to God's leading and recognizing His perfect knowledge and higher ways.

Moreover, in his letter to the Romans, the apostle Paul encourages believers by saying, "Do not conform yourselves to the patterns of this world but let your minds be transformed through renewal. "Then, you will have the ability to test and confirm what God's will is. His pleasing and perfect will (Romans 12;2, NIV). By seeking guidance from God and aligning our choices with wisdom, we break away from conforming to societal norms and embark on a transformative journey that unleashes our divine potential.

Throughout history, Christian writers have echoed these truths as they emphasize the importance of seeking God's guidance. A.W. Tozer beautifully captures this wisdom in his work "The Pursuit of God" by stating that "Finding God and continuously pursuing Him is the paradox of the soul's love." This paradoxical pursuit implies a journey of seeking God's guidance, which demonstrates our love for Him and our longing to align our choices with His divine wisdom.

C.S. Lewis, another Christian author, in his book "Mere Christianity " echoes this sentiment by explaining that both good things and bad things can be contagious. He suggests that if we want to feel warmth, we need to stand near a fire; if we're going to experience it, we must enter the water.

If you seek happiness, strength, inner peace and everlasting life, you must come close to it. Even immerse yourself in the source that possesses these qualities. Lewis emphasizes the importance of aligning ourselves with wisdom to truly experience the transformative power of God in our lives.

When we make decisions that are guided by wisdom, we not only unlock our own godly potential but also become vessels through which God's purposes can be fulfilled. As Charles H. Spurgeon, a known preacher from the 19th century, once said, "Trusting God when everything is going well doesn't require much faith; trusting Him during difficult times—that's true faith." Embracing God's guidance in decision-making may not always be effortless. It is during these moments of complete surrender and trust that we encounter divine blessings to their fullest extent and witness the realization of our own God-given abilities.

It is truly inspiring and transformative to seek God's guidance and align our decisions with wisdom. By doing so, we can unlock our divine potential in ways that go beyond human reasoning, societal norms and our limited understanding. The Bible and the teachings of Bible scholars and Christian authors consistently affirm the power of this approach. It encourages us to step out in faith, seek God's guidance and align our decisions with wisdom. It is through this alignment that we fully embrace the possibilities of our divine potential.

The journey we embark on shapes us as much as the answers we discover.

When we pursue Kingdom wisdom, it is essential to recognize that the journey itself has an impact on shaping who we are. The process of seeking moulds our spirit and guides us in making decisions. These profound words echo the timeless wisdom found within scripture and the teachings of Bible scholars and Christian writers.

As James reminds us in his epistle, "If any of you lacks wisdom, let him ask God, who gives generously to all without reproach, and it will be given him" (James 1:5 ESV). This verse serves as a reminder that wisdom is more than just a destination we reach; it is a gift from God that we actively pursue. The journey of seeking knowledge not only transforms us but also shapes our character, deepens our understanding and aligns our hearts with God's will.

In his book titled "The Pursuit of God ", A.W. Tozer beautifully expresses the significance of this journey in our pursuit of wisdom. He explains that when we have God as our treasure, we have everything in one. While earthly treasures may be withheld or enjoyed with moderation, they are never essential to our happiness (Tozer, 1948). Tozer's words highlight that the actual value lies not in reaching the destination but instead in the personal growth and transformation experienced while seeking God's wisdom.

Additionally, Timothy Keller emphasizes the importance of embracing the process of seeking wisdom amidst pain and suffering in her book "Walking with God Through Pain and Suffering." Keller states that although it is not a journey, it is during this process that we encounter God's presence and guidance most profoundly (Keller, 2013). This powerful reminder reminds us to embrace the challenges and difficulties we face in our journey, understanding that they play a role in shaping our character and strengthening our faith in God.

To conclude, seeking Kingdom wisdom is not simply about finding answers. Embarking on a transformative path that shapes our inner being and guides our choices. As we pursue knowledge, let us keep in mind the teachings of James, the insights of A.W. Tozer and the knowledge shared by Timothy Keller. May we wholeheartedly embrace the process of seeking, recognizing that it is within this journey that we encounter God's presence, His guidance and the transformation of our hearts.

God's wisdom acts as a guiding lamp rather than a distant star.

God's wisdom serves as a present guiding lamp that walks alongside us, ready to illuminate our path and provide divine certainty. It is not a star that can only be observed from afar; instead, it remains a constant presence we can seek with an open heart. This concept beautifully resonates within religious texts such as the Bible. It has been further explored by esteemed Bible scholars and Christian authors.

In the Psalms, the Psalmist beautifully expresses the idea that God's Word serves as a guiding light illuminating our path Psalm 119:105, NIV). This verse captures the essence of how seeking God's guidance with a heart brings clarity and direction to our lives.

John R.W. Stott, a known scholar of the Bible, further delves into this concept in his book "The Message of Psalms." He explains that the imagery of a lamp symbolizes how God's revealed Word offers guidance, protection and companionship to those who embrace it (Stott, 246). Stott emphasizes that when we rely on God's Word, we tap into a source of wisdom and take solace in knowing that we are not alone on our journey.

As followers of Christianity, we are encouraged to seek God's wisdom in our lives. When we approach Him with a heart and a willingness to receive His guidance, we are met with unwavering divine certainty. It is through this wisdom that we discover purpose, serenity and clear direction.

The idea that God's wisdom acts as an illuminating lamp rather than a distant star holds great power and inspiration. It serves as a reminder for us to wholeheartedly seek His guidance and trust in the certainty He provides. By delving into the words of Psalmists, studying insights from scholars like John R.W. Stott and exploring C.S. Lewis's allegorical depiction in "The Chronicles of Narnia ", we can gain a deeper comprehension of this truth. Let us embrace God's wisdom so it may light our path and guide us with assurance.

His wisdom perceives a work of art.

In the realm of divinity, decisions are not about setting boundaries but rather about expressing His purpose on the canvas of life. While we may perceive ambiguity, His wisdom perceives a work of art. This profound concept finds its exquisite embodiment in the masterpiece called 'Walking in His Ways, authored by Sarah Johnson, a devoted Christian writer. Through her words, Johnson inspires us to embrace God's guidance and have unwavering faith in His more excellent plan for our existence.

Described with eloquence by Johnson herself, God's perspective resembles that of an artist meticulously crafting a masterpiece. Just as an artist begins with a canvas brimming with endless possibilities and potential, God perceives our lives as an empty space where He can paint His divine calling. Often, we find ourselves grappling with decision-making because we are limited to seeing a few options ahead. However, God's wisdom surpasses our comprehension. He possesses a blueprint for each one of us and yearns to create a unique and enchanting portrait through our life journeys.

Johnson serves as a reminder that through unwavering faith, we can tap into God's wisdom and discern His calling amidst uncertainty. In life, we encounter choices without clear answers. We find ourselves torn between diverging paths and need to know which one to tread upon. "During times of confusion, we can seek solace in turning to God for guidance, understanding that He has a perspective. He recognizes the potential within each choice. Comprehends how it fits into His grand design. By seeking His will and attentively listening to His voice, we are able to make decisions that align with His plans for our lives.

The journey of discerning God's calling isn't always sailing, but it is undoubtedly worthwhile. Johnson shares her encounters of faithfully following God's guidance in her own life and how it has resulted in remarkable outcomes. She encourages us to release our fears and place our trust in God's leading when the path ahead seems unclear. Through her words, she kindly reminds us that God is ever faithful and will never abandon us.

As we navigate through life's trials, it is essential to remember that God's wisdom surpasses our understanding. We may encounter situations that appear insurmountable or come across decisions that need clear answers. However, Johnson serves as a reminder that God's ways are higher than ours, and His thoughts transcend our thoughts. In moments of uncertainty, finding solace in the knowledge that God sees the picture brings us peace and assurance that He will guide us accordingly.

In her book "Walking in His Ways " Sarah Johnson draws inspiration from narratives that exemplify this fundamental truth. She refers to the story of Joseph, who encountered challenges and uncertainties before realizing God's greater purpose for his life. Through Joseph's journey, Johnson underscores the significance of trust, patience and faithfulness in embracing God's calling. Like Joseph, we may encounter setbacks and detours along our paths, but rest assured that God remains unwavering in His intentions for our lives.

Walking in His Ways by Sarah Johnson is a captivating and motivational book that urges us to place our trust in God's wisdom when making decisions. Johnson's words serve as a reminder that our lives resemble canvases upon which God paints His calling through the choices we make. During moments of uncertainty, finding solace in the knowledge that God comprehends the picture and will guide us at just the right time can bring immense comfort. By embracing His guidance and placing our trust in His plans, we can lead lives that genuinely reflect His masterpiece.

Chapter Six

In His Kingdom Power

Accessing Supernatural Strength

In a world filled with chaos and uncertainty, there is a longing within us for a power that surpasses our own abilities. We yearn for strength to guide us through life's trials and challenges. This desire leads us to explore the pages of "Kingdom Power; accessing supernatural strength", an enlightening masterpiece designed to inspire and guide believers on their spiritual journey.

As we immerse ourselves in this captivating book, we are invited to explore the biblical principles that unlock the gateway to supernatural experiences. Esteemed Bible scholars and devoted Christian authors have contributed their wisdom and insights, weaving together revelations, timeless teachings and scriptural truths. Drawing inspiration from the words of renowned theologian A.W. Tozer, who stated, "The Holy Spirit is Gods Spirit, fully equal with both God the Father and God the Son... Every good work accomplished by believers in the power of the Spirit is ultimately done by God Himself " the author establishes a foundation, for understanding Kingdom Power.

In the chapter titled "Accessing Supernatural Strength", we find ourselves on the verge of a life-altering revelation. I seamlessly weave together the teachings of renowned Bible scholar Myles Munroe, who emphasized that we possess everything to fulfil our unique purpose. We are urged to delve into the depths of our God-given power and unleash it. As we progress through the pages, we are motivated to shed our self-imposed limitations and surrender to the strength bestowed upon us by God. Our souls are nourished by the wisdom imparted by luminaries like C.S. Lewis, who profoundly stated that true happiness and peace can only be found in connection with God.

I invite you into a realm where supernatural experiences abound as subsequent chapters explore dimensions of Kingdom Power. Drawing from a source of biblical truths, we gain enlightenment from the words of A.W. Pink, an esteemed American theologian and pastor who asserted that prayer is not about overcoming God's reluctance but embracing His willingness. These profound words echo the sentiment that prayer is the key to accessing God's supernatural strength within His Kingdom.

As we continue our journey through the "Kingdom Power "pages, we encounter applications and transformative insights from Joseph Prince, a well-known pastor and author from Singapore. He reminds us that when we wonder where God is, it's important to remember that the teacher is always quiet during the test. In moments of adversity, we realize that it is in our moments of weakness that God's power shines bright.

The culmination of this book can be found in its final chapter titled Unleashing the Kingdom within You. Here, we are reminded of the words spoken by T.D. Jakes is an author who emphasizes that we carry the Kingdom within ourselves. Like Christ, we can bring dominion and authority wherever life takes us. We are encouraged to embrace our potential and confidently walk in the supernatural strength bestowed upon us.

"Kingdom Power: Accessing Supernatural Strength" isn't just a book; it serves as an invitation, a guidebook and a source of divine wisdom. It urges us to cast aside doubts or fears and encourages us to grasp the power within us.

As we embark on this journey, we find inspiration in following the path laid out by our heavenly Father. By tapping into His strength, we can truly experience the richness and abundance of His Kingdom right here on earth.

Not in commanding others but in serving our divine purpose.

The understanding of Kingdom Power reveals a truth: real influence does not come from commanding others but from serving our divine purpose. Throughout history, humans have been captivated by the allure of power and control, believing they can achieve greatness by exerting authority over others. However, as Christian teachings remind us, true passion lies in serving others and fulfilling the unique purpose that God has bestowed upon us.

Rick Warren explores this concept extensively in his book "The Purpose Driven Life." According to Warren's insights, we are not mere accidents on this earth; God has designed a specific purpose for us. This notion aligns harmoniously with the understanding of Kingdom power. Striving to dominate and impose our will upon others, we should dedicate ourselves to discovering and fulfilling the individual calling that God has placed within us.

A remarkable illustration of this principle can be found in the life teachings of Jesus Christ as depicted in the Gospel of Mark. Through his actions and words, Jesus imparts lessons about authentic leadership and demonstrates that true greatness comes from humble service rather than a thirst for control.

Jesus teaches, "If anyone desires greatness, they must become a servant" (Mark 10:43). Jesus, the Son of God, did not come to rule over the world but to serve humanity. His ultimate act of service was sacrificing himself on the cross to redeem all of mankind. Jesus showed us the path to absolute power through his humility and selflessness.

Understanding the concept of Kingdom Power requires a shift in our mindset from one focused on domination to one centred around service. Seeking control and manipulation over others, our aim should be to bless and uplift them. As stated by the apostle Peter in his letter, "Each person should use their gifts received to serve others faithfully as stewards of God's diverse grace" (1 Peter 4:10). We tap into an incredible source of influence and power by embracing our calling and utilizing our talents to serve others.

The life story of Mother Teresa exemplifies someone who perfectly embodied Kingdom power. Through her love and unwavering dedication towards those living in extreme poverty, Mother Teresa transformed countless lives. She once expressed that while she alone couldn't change the world completely, she could create significant ripples by casting a stone across the waters. Mother Teresa recognized that true strength comes not from exerting control over others but from serving them with love and compassion.

Understanding the concept of Kingdom Power can completely transform our perspective on influence. By seeking dominance, we can profoundly impact by fulfilling our divine purpose. Drawing wisdom from the teachings of Jesus, the insights shared by authors like Rick Warren, and the inspiring example set by Mother Teresa, we are reminded that genuine power lies in selfless service. Let us strive to embrace our calling, serve others with love and empathy, and witness the profound influence that follows.

In a world driven by the pursuit of power and domination, it becomes crucial for believers to grasp the understanding of Kingdom power and its distinction from worldly notions of power. Kingdom power, rooted in wisdom and love, can transform lives, heal brokenness, and restore hope. By exploring scripture and insights offered by Christian authors, we gain a deeper understanding of the true essence of power. This inspires believers to shift their mindset regarding seeking influence and making an impact.

Renowned theologian and author John Piper delves into this distinction between the Kingdom and worldly power in his book "The Power of the Kingdom. "He highlights that the power of the Kingdom is not about using force or coercion. Instead, it is found in humility, servitude, and sacrificial love. Piper underscores that the actual demonstration of Kingdom power can be seen in the life of Jesus Christ, who willingly gave up His life for the redemption of humanity. God's true power was revealed through this act of submission and selflessness, surpassing sin and death. This self-sacrificing love lies at the heart of Kingdom power, inspiring believers to follow in Christ's footsteps and embrace a life characterized by humility and servanthood.

In line with this perspective, Beth Moore echoes a sentiment in her book "Breaking Free ", emphasizing that Kingdom power originates from a deep understanding of our identity in Christ. She explores how surrendering our desires and ambitions to align with God's divine will brings transformation. Moore encourages believers to seek God's power through prayer, seeking wisdom and discernment in every decision, trusting that His plans far surpass our own. She stresses that Kingdom power is not about success or dominance but instead revolves around establishing a profound connection with the Creator by surrendering our lives to His divine purpose and witnessing His supernatural work unfold.

In "Mere Christianity ", C.S. Lewis explores the relationship between power and human will. He introduces the idea that divine power doesn't diminish freedom but enhances it. Lewis suggests true passion lies in submitting our choice to God's will. He emphasizes that genuine power comes from obeying God's commandments and aligning our actions and desires with His love. By doing believers tap into the profound depths of God's power, causing a ripple effect of blessings and restoration in the world around them.

Comprehending Kingdom power necessitates a shift in mindset, breaking away from society's understanding of power. It involves embracing humility, servitude, and selfless love as pathways through which authentic power manifests itself. As believers, we are called to mirror Christ's character and serve as vessels for His transformative power. Through the wisdom and guidance writers provide, we are encouraged to align our lives with God's perfect plan while surrendering our personal ambitions and desires. This surrender unlocks opportunities to experience the encompassing power of the Creator of the universe flowing through us, bringing healing, restoration, and hope to a fractured world.

Embracing the wind of the Holy Spirit.

The concept of embracing the wind of the Holy Spirit may be familiar to many. Still, only a select few genuinely embrace its profound influence. It is a force that defies comprehension, displaying infinite and boundless strength. Our lives undergo unimaginable transformations when we unlock this power and tap into the kingdom power bestowed by God. This power demands unwavering faith, urging us to seek and act while surrendering our own desires to the divine wisdom of God.

In his book "The Power of the Holy Spirit", Billy Graham delves into the life-altering impact of the Holy Spirit on believers. Graham elaborates on how the Holy Spirit empowers us to lead lives that please God, overcome obstacles, and radiate God's love worldwide.

Graham's words serve as a reminder that the strength of the Holy Spirit should not be kept to us but shared and utilized to bring about positive change in the lives of others.

When we fully embrace the influence of the Holy Spirit, it is crucial to acknowledge that our faith is what unlocks its power within us. In A.W. Tozer's book, "The Pursuit of God", he emphasizes that faith is the key that opens doors to experiences. Through faith, we can believe in what may seem impossible, trust in what cannot be seen, and obediently follow God's will. Tozer's words encourage us to nurture an unwavering faith that remains steadfast despite challenging circumstances.

Once we possess faith as our guiding force, we are called upon to seek and align ourselves with God's will. In Rick Warren's book, "The Purpose Driven Life", he discusses the significance of seeking God's will and living a life that harmonizes with it. Warren highlights that when we prioritize seeking God first, His wisdom and power flow through us, empowering us to make decisions and take actions guided by His spirit.

Warren reminds us that our lives hold significance and purpose when we willingly embrace God's plan and allow His power to manifest through us.

Surrendering is the step in accessing the boundless potential of God's wisdom. In C.S. Lewis's book "Mere Christianity", he delves into the notion of surrender and the transformative changes that occur when we wholeheartedly yield ourselves to God. Lewis explains that surrendering to God's wisdom entails releasing our desires, intentions and ambitions and granting God complete control. By relinquishing our agendas and yielding to God's divine will, we open ourselves up to His exclusive power and wisdom. Lewis emphasizes that genuine fulfilment and purpose are discovered by surrendering to God's flawless blueprint.

Embracing the guidance of the Holy Spirit and unlocking the unlimited strength of heavenly authority demands faith-seeking, acting, and surrendering to God's wisdom. As we immerse ourselves in literature by Christian authors like Billy Graham, A.W. Tozer, Rick Warren, or C.S. Lewis himself, their writings inspire us while urging us to fully tap into the power and wisdom bestowed upon us by God.

Let us have the courage to embrace our faith wholeheartedly, seeking God's guidance and fully trusting in His purpose. By doing so, we will witness the profound influence of the Holy Spirit and spread God's love and mercy throughout the world.

We are called to go beyond mere observation.

To truly understand and experience the power of God's Kingdom, we are called to go beyond mere observation. Instead, we are encouraged to participate and become influential agents of divine change. By embracing the range of supernatural abilities bestowed upon us, we can witness first-hand the extent of His grace through miracles, strengthen our faith through spiritual battles, and impact society. This essay takes a dive into this incredible journey, drawing inspiration from esteemed Christian authors who have paved the way with their profound and captivating stories.

As we open our hearts and minds to the awe-inspiring power of God's Kingdom, we begin to see how His boundless grace can touch every aspect of our lives. Mark Batterson's book "The Circle Maker "teaches us the importance of persistently seeking God's intervention by using an ancient Jewish practice known as drawing circles.

By trusting God's miraculous power, we open ourselves to His grace flowing into every aspect of our lives. It is essential to understand that His miracles are not confined to times but are available even today.

To fully embrace the power of God's Kingdom, we must engage in a battle against the forces of darkness that aim to hinder our growth and limit our impact on the world. In his book "War in Heaven, War on Earth ", Derek Prince reminds us that our fight is not against flesh and blood but against spiritual powers. Equipped with the armour of God and armed with prayer and scripture, we can overcome the enemy's strategies. Emerge victorious as we seek to manifest God's Kingdom power.

Throughout our journey on earth, we have opportunities to sow seeds of divine influence within societal structures. In "The Irresistible Revolution ", Shane Claiborne challenges us to live out our faith by actively engaging with marginalized communities and advocating for social justice. He emphasizes that serving others and working towards transformation is essential to manifesting God's Kingdom power here, on earth.

By acting and embodying Christ's love and compassion, we can bring change to our communities and institutions.

In our quest for the power of God's Kingdom, it is not enough to watch from the sidelines; we must actively engage and allow His supernatural power to work through us. Bill Johnson's book "When Heaven Invades Earth "reminds us that we are called to carry God's presence and unleash His power wherever we go. By nurturing a relationship with God and letting His Spirit flow through us, we become channels through which His supernatural power can touch the lives of others. This requires us to be receptive and obedient, stepping out in faith when faced with opposition.

Embracing the range of God's Kingdom power is a transformative journey beyond passive observation; it calls for active participation in His work of grace, faith, and influence. As we pursue miracles, witness the extent of God's grace, engage in spiritual warfare, and sow seeds of divine influence, we can tangibly experience supernatural power at work.

Drawing inspiration from Christian authors such as Mark Batterson, Derek Prince, Shane Claiborne and Bill Johnson, we are encouraged to embrace the wisdom of God and reflect His transformative power in our lives. Let us wholeheartedly accept this calling and become influential channels of change, spreading light, hope and love to a world longing for it.

It should encompass a profound commitment to prayer, fasting, and obedience.

In a world characterized by chaos and uncertainty, it becomes essential for believers to seek solace, strength, and guidance through their faith. Our spiritual journey should surpass superficial encounters; rather, it should encompass a profound commitment to prayer, fasting, and obedience exercises that strengthen our faith and maintain an open mindset. We can access an abundant source of supernatural strength by opening ourselves up to the power of God's Kingdom instead of merely knocking at its door. Like an ocean with no boundaries or limitations—endless in its depth—we can dive fearlessly into the realm of God's wisdom and tap into His limitless power. This allows us to witness transformations unfolding within our own lives.

We will delve into the significance of establishing a deeper connection with God, drawing insights and wisdom from influential Christian writers.

Prayer serves as the link that connects us to God, enabling us to seek His guidance and insight. In his book "Altar Ego; Becoming Who God Says You Are, " Craig Groeschel emphasizes the crucial role of prayer as a practice. According to Groeschel, by embracing prayer, we open ourselves up to a spiritual awakening that aligns us with the divine power of the Kingdom. Additionally, fasting brings us closer to God by relinquishing desires and focusing on matters of the spirit. In her book "Fasting: Opening the Door to a More Intimate, More Powerful Relationship with God ", Jantzen Franklin guides readers in understanding that fasting, combined with prayer, leads to divine intervention and extraordinary breakthroughs.

Adhering obediently to God's commands unlocks His power within our lives. In his book "When Heaven Invades Earth; A Practical Guide to a Life of Miracles" Bill Johnson emphasizes that genuine obedience stems from our love and trust in God. By obeying His commands without reservation, we align ourselves with His divine purposes and open ourselves up to experiencing His supernatural power. We demonstrate our faith and willingness to surrender by obeying, allowing God to work powerfully through us.

Faith plays a role in our relationship with God, enabling us to receive His blessings and witness miracles in His name. In his book "Faith That Prevails ", Smith Wigglesworth encourages believers to nurture an unwavering faith. He emphasizes that faith is cultivated through studying and reflecting on the Word of God, persevering in prayer, and taking steps of obedience. We deepen our connection with God by practising these exercises that strengthen our faith. Invite His supernatural power to manifest in our lives.

Maintaining a minded attitude is critical to accessing God's supernatural power. In her book "Battlefield of the Mind " Joyce Meyer emphasizes the importance of renewing our minds and guarding against negative influences. By being receptive to God's guidance, revelation and transformation, we can experience the extent of His power and divine wisdom. A-minded approach liberates us from doubt, worry, and fear while allowing God's supernatural strength to flow freely into our lives. Embracing prayer fasting, obedience, faith-building exercises, and a minded mindset is essential for unlocking the extraordinary power of God.

By immersing ourselves in the depths of His love and wisdom, we position ourselves to witness miracles, divine interventions, and a pouring out of His grace. As followers of Christ, let us embrace the knowledge shared by authors such as Craig Groeschel, Jentezen Franklin, Bill Johnson, Smith Wigglesworth and Joyce Meyer. May their teachings ignite our passion to unlock the door to Kingdom Power with unwavering faith and wise actions. Remember that God's supernatural strength is not a source but an expansive ocean waiting for us to explore.

It is not mere capability or ability. It is a divine responsibility.

Kingdom power is more than ability; it is a sacred responsibility. Let us humbly and selflessly steward it as a guiding light for others. True godly power lies in humble stewardship rather than mere possession.

This inspiring story will delve into the concept that Kingdom Power goes beyond mere capability; it is a divine duty. It should be entrusted to those who are willing to guide others humbly and selflessly with it. True godly power can be found in humble stewardship rather than simply possessing it alone.

Let's embark on this journey as we seek wisdom from Christian writers who have shed light on this subject, guiding us towards a deeper understanding of our role in the Kingdom.

As we explore the depths of this thought-provoking idea, it becomes clear that genuine kingdom power is not about using authority for gain or selfish ambitions. Instead, it presents an opportunity to serve others and impact their lives. Christian writer John Maxwell beautifully captures this concept by saying,

"Leadership is not about being in control; it's about taking care of those under your care" (Maxwell, 1998). From this perspective, we realize that godly power comes with a responsibility to lead with empathy, compassion and a sincere desire to uplift those around us.

The concept of stewarding kingdom power with humility profoundly resonates with the teachings of Jesus Christ. In His ministry, Jesus exemplified the essence of godly power by washing His disciple's feet—a profound act demonstrating humility and service (John 13:1-17).

Christian writer and theologian Oswald Chambers reflects on this idea, expressing that our service should resemble Jesus Himself so much that others might ask if we are also from Galilee (Chambers, 1935). When we embrace humility, we not only fulfil the sacred duty entrusted to us but also inspire others to seek and follow the path of servant leadership.

When we exercise power in a manner with selflessness at its core, we embody the essence of Christ's teachings. These teachings emphasize love and caring for others. As C.S. Lewis eloquently puts it, humility is not about thinking less of oneself but of oneself less (Lewis, 2006). As we pursue power within His Kingdom, we are called to set aside our desires and instead prioritize the needs and well-being of those we serve. Doing so makes our radiance undeniable—a light that draws others toward the transformative beauty of godly power.

True Godly power is not just intended to uplift ourselves; it serves as a guiding light for others. Through humble stewardship of our control, we can illuminate their paths, leading them towards their divine potential.

Renowned Christian writer Rick Warren beautifully expresses this viewpoint, asserting that true humility involves not diminishing one's self-worth but shifting the focus away from oneself and towards others (Warren, 2002). By acknowledging the responsibility that accompanies the power of the Kingdom, we can motivate and empower others to uncover and embrace their unique talents.

When contemplating the duty tied to kingdom power, it is crucial to remember that it should not be seen as something to possess or boast about. Instead, it should be regarded as a gift to be shared with modesty and selflessness. By following the teachings and examples set by Christ as elucidated by Christian authors like John Maxwell, Oswald Chambers, C.S. Lewis and Rick Warren himself, we can genuinely embody the essence of godly authority. Let us strive to steward our kingdom power by taking on the responsibility of serving others while inspiring and guiding them towards their own divine potential. In doing so, we become radiant sources of illumination in a world desperately craving godly wisdom, love and transformation.

Chapter Seven

In His Kingdom Stories

Doors, Windows, Rope Holders, and Basket Cases.

When we delve into the metaphoric of doors, windows, rope holders and basketcases, we uncover an incredibly captivating narrative that sheds light on the untold lessons of the Kingdom of God. Through these representations, we can establish a deep connection that inspires and enlightens us on our spiritual journey. As we explore further, we discover hidden truths that encourage us to embrace our role as vessels of divine love, grace and redemption.

Doors act as gateways that beckon us to step into realms or leave behind what is familiar. They symbolize opportunities for growth, learning and transformation. In Matthew 7:7, Jesus urges us to "ask and you shall receive; seek and you shall find; knock and it will be opened unto you." Here, knocking on the door represents not a physical action but a metaphor for seeking divine guidance and wisdom. The door represents the depths of God's love and grace awaiting those who earnestly desire to dwell in His Kingdom.

Windows allow us to glimpse beyond the confines of our surroundings. They remind us to look beyond the limitations of this world and perceive the spiritual realm. In 1 Corinthians 13:12, Paul expresses that our current understanding is limited using the metaphor of seeing a reflection in a mirror. However, he anticipates a time when we will have knowledge and see things face to face. This verse highlights our comprehension of our earthly existence. Windows serves as a reminder for us to adopt a perspective enabling us to appreciate the beauty of God's Kingdom and connect with divine truths that surpass our human limitations.

Rope holders play a role as support systems, ensuring that our spiritual journey remains steady and secure. Ecclesiastes 4:12 states that while one person may be overpowered alone, two individuals can defend themselves better by standing. A cord made of three strands is robust and not easily broken. This metaphor emphasizes the significance of fellowship and community among believers, underscoring our interdependence within the body of Christ. Similar to how ropes provide stability and strength by holding onto something, these relationships offer us peace and strength as we navigate life's challenges while remaining connected to God.

The idea of being a basket case refers to acknowledging our brokenness and weakness before God, recognizing that we need His transformation and redemption. In 2 Corinthians 12:9, it says, "My grace is sufficient for you for my power is made perfect in weakness." When we embrace our vulnerabilities, we become channels through which God's power can flow. By accepting our imperfections, we allow God's grace to work mightily in us. This reminds us that our weaknesses can be transformed into strengths that bring glory to His Kingdom.

The story of doors, windows, rope holders and basketcases reveals the parables of the Kingdom of God. It takes us on a journey connected divinely. When we approach opportunities with faith, like opening doors, seek perception, like looking through windows, rely on fellow believers as trustworthy rope holders, and surrender our weaknesses as basketcases—our lives align with God's eternal plan. Through these metaphors, we are reminded of the potential within us to share godly wisdom, love and redemption in a world longing for spiritual nourishment.

By embracing the connection, we unlock the power to serve, inspire and bring positive change to others' lives. It is through our unity with the Kingdom of God that we truly discover the richness of life's purpose.

In His Kingdom an open door reveals.

Exploring the concept of the Kingdom of God as a door reveals a captivating narrative. We will delve into its meaning and uncover profound wisdom hidden within. Embracing this perspective provides inspiration and motivation to embrace the Kingdom of God, allowing it to profoundly transform our lives.

Throughout accounts, doors have often represented passages, transitions and opportunities. In Revelation 3:20, Jesus speaks these words; "Behold I stand at the door and knock. If anyone hears my voice and opens the door, I will come into him. Eat with him and he with me." This verse beautifully illustrates Jesus patiently waiting at the door of our hearts, gently inviting us to welcome Him in. By opening ourselves up to Jesus's presence, we ask the Kingdom of God to dwell within us—bringing about a transformation in every aspect of our lives.

The idea of a door also represents inclusivity and invitation. Jesus emphasized repeatedly that the Kingdom of God is not limited to a few but is accessible to anyone willing to embrace it. In Matthew 7:7-8 Jesus encourages us by saying, "Ask and you will receive; seek and you will find; knock and the door will be opened to you. Everyone who asks receives everyone who seeks finds and for those who knock the door will be opened." This passage serves as a reminder that the door to God's Kingdom is always open for those earnestly seeking Him.

Furthermore, the symbolism of a door invites us to step out of our comfort zones and embark on a transformative journey. In John 10:9, Jesus declares, "I am the door. If anyone enters through me, they will be. Freely move in and out and find nourishment." Jesus not only serves as the gateway but also provides nourishment and abundant life that awaits beyond the threshold. Embracing the Kingdom of God as a door urges us to have faith in what lies ahead on this path—knowing that it is far greater than anything we leave behind.

Looking at it from a viewpoint, an open door can also symbolize an opportunity to extend God's love and grace to others. In the book of 2 Corinthians 2:12, the apostle Paul writes about his visit to Troas and how a door was opened for him in the Lord as he shared the gospel of Christ. Paul's use of this metaphor emphasizes the chances that God presents to us, enabling us to spread His message of hope and salvation. By recognizing these doors, we can confidently step forward and let the Kingdom of God impact others through our words and actions.

The concept of a door captures a motivating and uplifting perspective on the Kingdom of God. Understanding that Jesus stands at the door of our hearts, patiently waiting for our invitation, invites us to unravel its symbolism and embrace God's transformative love. This perspective encourages us to take steps in faith, knowing that the abundant life offered by Jesus surpasses anything we may leave behind. Additionally, the imagery of a door serves as a reminder for us to be attentive to opportunities that God places in our path so that we can share His love with others.

Therefore, let's uncover the entrance, reveal the underlying symbolism, and invite the Kingdom of God to open our doors, minds and hearts. This will lead us towards a perspective on the incredible love and grace of God.

In His Kingdom allow us to see an open window.

Throughout life, we often encounter opportunities that possess the potential to shape our future. These opportunities act as windows that offer a glimpse into a world filled with possibilities. When we embrace the teachings of the Kingdom of God with a mind and heart, we come to realize that it is not just a destination but also an opportunity for personal growth, transformation and fulfilment. Through this journey, we will delve into how the Kingdom of God resembles an opportunity-filled window that unlocks our true potential and unveils secrets capable of inspiring us to take a leap of faith and embrace the divine path before us.

The Kingdom of God possesses a power that allows us to unlock our hidden potential. Similar to how sunlight floods into a room through a window, the Kingdom of God illuminates the depths within us by revealing our strengths, talents and passions.

As we surrender ourselves to God's will, we tap into a source of grace that leads us towards unlocking our true potential.

Jesus, who serves as the foundation of God's Kingdom, exemplified this principle throughout His ministry. He nurtured the abilities of His disciples, empowering them to become influencers in people's lives. When Peter took a step and walked on water, he personally experienced the incredible potential that resides within us when we embrace the opportunities presented by God's Kingdom (Matthew 14:29).

God's Kingdom holds secrets of transforming our lives. Like a window allows us to see beyond our physical limitations, the Kingdom of God reveals spiritual truths that surpass our earthly existence. The Scriptures offer wisdom guiding us towards a life that aligns with God's purpose.

Proverbs 3:5-6 reminds us to trust in the Lord and acknowledge that His ways often transcend our understanding. When we place our trust in God's Kingdom, we unlock the secret of surrender and comprehend that His plans exceed our own desires.

By surrendering control and embracing the guidance of power, we expose ourselves to a wide range of possibilities that would otherwise remain concealed.

Taking a step forward in faith is akin to opening a window to opportunities. When we perceive the realm of God as our personal gateway to potential, we take a leap of faith, firmly believing in the authenticity of God's promises and his benevolent intentions for us (Jeremiah 29:11).

Abraham's journey serves as an exemplification of venturing through the door of opportunity presented by God. When God summoned Abraham to depart from his homeland, Abraham placed unwavering trust in the Lord's assurance that he would become the progenitor of a nation. Despite his age and lack of offspring, Abraham took that courageous leap, knowing that within the Kingdom of God lay provisions for all his necessities. Through his obedience, Abraham emerged as the forefather of nations, leaving behind an enduring legacy that inspires us all to place our trust in God's open doors (Genesis 12).

A window of opportunity to speak at a conference.

In life, there are moments when divine providence presents us with windows of opportunity, leading us into territories where we are called upon to embrace faith and follow divine guidance.

It was a remarkable moment when I unexpectedly received an invitation to speak at a conference of pastors and leaders in Africa. My heart filled with joy as I recognized this as the chance to fulfil my calling from God. Spreading His Word and sharing His love with others. However, doubts and concerns surfaced from those to me, including my own family. They questioned the authenticity of the invitation, wondering if those who invited me were pastors. These worries clouded my mind. This caused some hesitation.

Nevertheless, I firmly believed that God's plans surpass human understanding, and He had purposefully presented this opportunity to me. Despite feeling discouraged, I decided to step out in faith and embark on an incredible journey to Africa. I knew that the path ahead might seem daunting. My unwavering belief in God's guidance and provision gave me the strength to move forward. Proverbs 3:5-6 became my anchor, reminding me to trust in the Lord with all my heart and not rely on my own understanding. As I submitted myself to Him in every aspect of my life, I knew He would make my path clear and straight (NIV). With this assurance, I entrusted all my fears and uncertainties to God, aware that His plans were far greater than any doubts I had.

Upon setting foot in Africa, I was captivated by its culture, warm hospitality and the remarkable spiritual atmosphere that embraced the land. It was evident that this divine journey was orchestrated by God as soon as I started interacting with pastors and leaders. Their authenticity and sincerity revealed a passion for doing God's work. All doubts and anxieties melted away as it became clear that I had been led to a gathering of men and women of God.

Embracing this opportunity to share the Word of God brought about a transformation within myself. The fire of the Holy Spirit burned intensely within me, igniting a sense of conviction and passion whenever I spoke.

I came to realize that ministry goes beyond preaching from a pulpit when I was in Africa. I witnessed transformations, healed hearts, and united communities through the power of God's Word. This experience became a moment for me, igniting a deep desire to continue spreading the gospel and making a positive impact wherever God may lead me.

Taking hold of the opportunity to go to Africa was genuinely life-changing as it allowed me to trust in God's guidance in times of doubt and uncertainty. This decision has profoundly influenced my ministry, reigniting my passion for the work of the Holy Spirit. We must never forget that when God presents an opportunity, we should not hesitate but step out in faith, fully trusting His plans for our lives. As Psalm 37:4 reminds us, "Delight yourself in the Lord. He will give you the desires of your heart" (NIV). Let us place our trust in God's love and allow Him to shape our paths as we rely on His wisdom and guidance.

The Kingdom of God calls upon us to awaken ourselves to the opportunities it offers. Tapping into our abilities, unravelling hidden truths, and igniting a sense of belief grants us the chance to embark on a profound journey. As we embrace the realm of God, welcoming wisdom and guidance into our lives, we can surpass our limitations and embrace a life filled with spiritual fulfilment.

Let us not underestimate the significance of the Kingdom of God as a gateway to possibilities. It is through this perspective that we can genuinely uncover our purpose, unleash our authentic potential, and draw inspiration to navigate the trials of life. By placing our trust in God's plan and taking those faithful leaps forward, we will witness extraordinary doors opening. We will see windows being sunlight-flooded with opportunities within the Kingdom of God that were beyond our wildest imagination.

The Significance of rope holders

Throughout our lives, we often face moments of difficulty that test our limits. These challenging times can leave us feeling overwhelmed, vulnerable and uncertain. However, in the Kingdom of God, we are never alone. God places individuals, often unsung heroes known as supporters, rope holders or allies, in our lives to offer guidance and support during these trying moments. These silent champions play a role in our spiritual growth by ensuring that we achieve success while embracing the support provided by God.

The concept of rope holders can be traced back to the account of Moses. When the Israelites faced their trial battling against the Amalekites, Moses ascended a hill with the staff of God held firmly in his hands. As long as Moses raised his hands high, the Israelites would prevail over their enemies. However, whenever fatigue set in his hands, it gave an advantage to the enemy forces. Recognizing the importance of assistance and encouragement, during times, Aaron and Hur stood to be a rope holder on either side of Moses, holding up his weary hands until sunset (Exodus 17:8-13).

This powerful story teaches us that each one of us needs rope holders throughout our journey. Supporters are those individuals who stand by us unwaveringly, providing support and encouragement when circumstances become overwhelming.

They silently guide us towards success by supporting us through prayer, lending an ear to listen, and offering wisdom and guidance when we find ourselves unsure of the way forward.

To fully embrace the support that God provides during life's moments, it is crucial to acknowledge and accept the individuals whom God has placed in our lives as rope holders. These rope holders can be our parents, siblings, friends, pastors, mentors or even strangers who cross our paths at the right time. They serve as a reflection of God's love and grace, providing us with the strength to overcome challenges and strengthen our faith.

In order to truly embrace God's support, we must cultivate a heart characterized by humility. While we may possess strength, talent and resources on our own accord, we do not intend to face life battles alone. The Apostle Paul reminds us of this truth in his letter to the Philippians when he urges us, saying, "Do nothing out of ambition or vain conceit. Rather in humility value others, above yourselves" (Philippians 2:3). By humbling ourselves in this manner, we create opportunities for God to work through our rope holders so they can fulfil their purpose within our lives.

To experience the presence of God during challenging times, it's essential to reach out to those who can provide support. Sometimes, we may hesitate to ask for help due to the fear of being judged or rejected. However, we must remember that the people who support us are not meant to replace God but rather serve as His instruments of grace. By sharing our struggles, doubts and fears with these individuals, we allow them to come alongside us and offer the assistance we need.

Moreover, embracing God's support in moments necessitates being open and vulnerable. We need to set aside our pride and let our supporters see the depths of our challenges. In this vulnerability, we create space for God's healing, restoration and blessings to enter our lives. The Apostle Peter encourages us in 1 Peter 5:6-7 by saying, "yourselves under Gods mighty hand so that he may lift you up at the right time. Cast all your anxieties on him because he cares for you."

Individuals are like unsung heroes within God's Kingdom; they guide us towards success by offering unwavering support and guidance during life's most challenging moments. Acknowledging and embracing the help of God during times requires humility, communication and vulnerability. We must not underestimate the role that our rope holders play in our lives as they demonstrate God's love and grace. As we accept their support, we draw closer to God, experiencing His strength and triumph as we navigate life's brutal battles.

When Rope Holders Release Their Grip

Life is a journey filled with ups and downs, successes and failures. Along our path of growth and service, there may be moments when those we trust the most, our "rope holders," let go. These individuals play a role in providing us with support, guidance and encouragement as we face the challenges that come with our calling. However, when they unexpectedly exit from our lives, it can leave us feeling confused, doubtful and even hopeless. During these trying times, it is essential to find solace in wisdom and recognize that God's plan often holds hidden opportunities for growth and renewed purpose.

When influential leaders or rope holders release their grip on the rope of support for us, it is natural to question God's plan for our ministry. It's natural to ask why God allowed this problematic situation to occur, especially when everything seemed to be going well. However, these hardships present us with opportunities for self-reflection, personal growth and a deepening reliance on our faith. In moments of challenge, God intends to teach us lessons that will equip us for even greater endeavours. A passage from Romans 5:3-4 reminds us that we can find joy in the midst of suffering because it produces perseverance, which leads to the development of character and ultimately brings hope.

When facing disappointment and despair, it becomes crucial for us to refocus on purpose and calling that God has entrusted upon our lives. Reflecting on our motivations for pursuing our ministry can reignite our passion and reinforce our determination to keep moving forward. It's essential to remember that although we may plan our paths in life, it is ultimately the Lord who establishes each step we take (Proverbs 16:9). Even when unexpected detours arise along our journey, we can trust that God has a plan.

During these times, we need to maintain a strong connection with God through fervent prayer, devoted study of His Word and seeking wise counsel from fellow believers. By surrendering ourselves to His wisdom, we allow Him to guide us along the right path while providing the strength needed to persevere.

The book of James encourages us to seek wisdom from God, who generously grants it to anyone who asks without any judgment. Putting our trust in His guidance can lead us to have a renewed vision for our ministry and an unwavering reliance on Him as the source of support.

When we see rope holders letting go, it serves as a reminder that change is an unavoidable part of life and ministry. Resisting or grieving over the loss of our rope holders, we should embrace the opportunity to engage with new individuals and different perspectives. It is through these transitions that God introduces viewpoints, fosters innovation, and prepares us for unexpected opportunities. Proverbs 27:17 reminds us that "as iron sharpens iron so one person sharpens another." New connections can bring insights and strengthen our determination to faithfully serve God.

Though it may be disheartening when rope holders let go, we can find comfort in knowing that through every trial, God is refining us. These experiences push us to become more resilient, more surrendered to His plan, and more reliant on His wisdom. In moments of despair, let us turn towards God because He holds all the inspiration, encouragement and godly wisdom we seek.

As we persevere and continue to have faith in His guidance, we will be astonished by the ways in which He brings people into our lives who support us and lead us to achieve things we never thought possible.

In His Kingdom embrace those basket case moments.

Throughout our journey through life, we come across challenges and difficulties that often make us feel overwhelmed and hopeless. However, when we embrace these moments with unwavering faith in the Kingdom of God, it can bring us closer to growth and a profound transformation. This part of our journey explores the nature of God's Kingdom, its unexpected methods of rescue and its remarkable ability to turn challenging situations into blessings.

The Kingdom of God, as Jesus proclaimed it, challenges understanding. It overturns society's standards and expectations by embracing those who are humble, weak and burdened with sorrow. It is through these perceived moments of vulnerability or being a "basket case" that the true power of God can be fully experienced. As the Apostle Paul affirms, "when I am at my point then I truly find strength" (2 Corinthians 12:10).

How God's Kingdom Rescues Us from Despair." In Paul's letter to the Corinthians, he shares an incident where he was safely lowered in a basket from a window in a wall, managing to escape capture. The passage from 2 Corinthians 11:33 states, ". I was lowered in a basket from a window in the wall and slipped through his hands." This moment not only signifies Paul's physical rescue but also highlights the transformative power of God's Kingdom. Just as Paul found deliverance from danger, we, too, can discover redemption from our difficult situations through divine intervention.

The Kingdom of Gods Surprising Rescue Methods. God's Kingdom doesn't rely on strength or conventional approaches to bring about change. It often operates in surprising ways that defy human logic. As seen in the story of Moses, there was a moment when he was placed in a basket and sent down the Nile River. However, through this seemingly desperate act, God worked out His divine plan and elevated Moses to become an influential leader who delivered His people from captivity.

In Acts 9:25, there is an incident where the apostle Paul manages to escape capture by being lowered in a basket from a window. This act, directed and rescued by God, represents His control over our lives. Sometimes, when we feel trapped and helpless, God can guide us through the narrowest of openings, freeing us from the grip of our circumstances.

From Helplessness to Hope.

The Perspective of the Kingdom of God on Being in a Difficult Situation Although feeling like a basket case may make us feel powerless and unimportant, the Kingdom of God brings about a change in how we see things. It challenges us to view our weaknesses as opportunities for experiencing God's grace and strength. By placing our faith in Him, we can find hope in the power of His Kingdom.

When we embrace those moments where we feel like basket cases with faith and surrender to the influence of the Kingdom of God, it can lead to significant spiritual growth and empowerment. Through examples and teachings found in narratives, we witness how the Kingdom operates with unexpected methods of rescue and can turn our struggles into blessings. By acknowledging God's sovereignty over our lives amidst challenging circumstances, we can discover hope, strength and redemption. As we place our trust in the loving care of God, we are empowered to rise above challenging moments and experience the richness of His Kingdom here on earth.

When I think about closing this chapter, it reminds me of all the opportunities that have presented themselves throughout my life. Initially, these opportunities may have appeared daunting or even impossible to pursue. However, as I reflect on my journey, I realize that each option represents a chance for growth, transformation and positive change. Some of these opportunities required courage and faith, while others demanded persistence and determination. Nevertheless, despite the obstacles and uncertainties I faced, I embraced each one with unwavering trust in God's plans for my life.

As I turned the doorknob of book writing education, I stepped into a room filled with knowledge and exploration. It was within this space that I discovered my passion for learning, an eagerness to broaden my horizons, and a commitment to strive for excellence in all aspects of my life. This door held the key to unlocking my potential. Equipped me with the necessary skills to make a meaningful impact in this world. Through work and dedication, I soared beyond what I thought possible by surpassing my own expectations and serving as an inspiration for others to follow.

Another door that called out to me was the doorway leading towards relationships and connections.

Inside this room, I met some remarkable individuals who became my pillars of support – the unwavering believers in me even when I doubted myself. They provided me with guidance, encouragement and love, lifting my spirits during moments of despair and celebrating my victories. Their presence in my life taught me the significance of surrounding myself with influences and nurturing meaningful relationships.

In one corner of this room, I stumbled upon a door labelled "basket cases - experiences that tested me." Initially hesitant to open it, I feared the pain and heartache that might lie behind me. However, as I summoned the courage to step inside, I realized that it was within these experiences that actual growth awaited me; they deepened my reliance on God. These moments of struggle honed my character, shaped my values and refined my faith. They imparted lessons – finding strength amidst adversity, embracing vulnerability, and placing trust in God's unwavering love and grace.

As I bring this chapter to a close, the words of Christian author C.S. Lewis echo in my mind; "There are better things ahead, than any we leave behind." My journey has taught me the power of perseverance, resilience and unshakable faith.

The future that lies ahead holds opportunities waiting for you to explore and seize. Embrace these possibilities with bravery and confidence. Surround yourself with individuals who will encourage and uplift you. Don't shy away from experiences that come your way, as they are the ones that shape you into the person you were meant to be. As you embark on the chapter of your journey, remember that your story is still unfolding, with God's wisdom and guidance leading you every step of the way.

CHAPTER EIGHT

IN HIS KINGDOM PROVISION

FINDING COMFORT IN GOD'S FAITHFULNESS

Finding peace and security can often be tricky in a world of uncertainty and challenges. Health crises, financial difficulties, and unexpected setbacks can disorient and overwhelm us. However, there is a source of hope that goes beyond our understanding and provides a foundation for our lives. It is the assurance we find in Finding Comfort in God's Faithfulness, known as Kingdom Provision. In this narrative, we delve into the essence of Kingdom Provision by drawing on the wisdom of Bible scholars and Christian authors. We aim to inspire, encourage, and instil the confidence to navigate life's trials.

Throughout the pages of the Bible, we encounter stories that showcase God's unwavering faithfulness in providing for His people. From His provision of manna during their time in the wilderness (Exodus 16:4) to multiplying bread and fish to feed the hungry (Matthew 14:13-21), we witness His incredible work. Yet God's faithfulness isn't limited solely to meeting needs; it extends to every aspect of our lives. As Paul writes in Philippians 4:19, ". My God will meet all your needs according to his glorious riches, in Christ Jesus. "This reminder emphasizes that God's provision is not a one-time occurrence but an ongoing relationship based on trust and reliance on Him.

According to Bible scholar John MacArthur, God's provision depends not on circumstances' ups and downs but on His unchanging character. We acknowledge our belief in His nature when we believe in God's faithfulness. It is a recognition that He remains the same yesterday, today, and forever (Hebrews 13:8). Christian writer Timothy Keller affirms, "God's faithfulness does not rely on our circumstances but on His love and mercy." We can find comfort in knowing that our Heavenly Father will never abandon us (Deuteronomy 31:6) and that His provision surpasses our earthly limitations.

Finding Comfort in God's faithfulness also requires participation from us. Kingdom Provision is not merely accepting circumstances passively; it involves surrendering our fears, worries and doubts. By letting go of self-reliance, we create space for God to work within and through us. Christian author A.W. Tozer explains that genuine faith rests upon the character of God. Doesn't demand further proof beyond the moral perfections of the One who cannot deceive. This surrender demonstrates our confidence in God's character and willingness to embrace His promises when facing challenges.

Furthermore, Kingdom Provision Finding Comfort in God's Faithfulness encourages us to adopt a mindset centred on God's kingdom. As Jesus teaches in Matthew 6:33, "Seek first the kingdom of God and His righteousness, and all these things will be added to you." This perspective urges us to prioritize our relationship with God above everything. When we align our hearts with His purposes, we witness an outpouring of provision that surpasses what we could expect on Earth. As Bible scholar Warren W. Wiersbe suggests, "Provision comes as a result of seeking the provider." When we genuinely seek after God and His kingdom, we realize that His faithfulness extends beyond meeting our material needs—it also encompasses our spiritual growth and transformation.

Kingdom Provision: Finding Comfort in God's Faithfulness unveils a wellspring of hope and assurance. Drawing from the wisdom of Bible scholars and

Christian authors, we discover that God's faithfulness is unwavering; it goes beyond our circumstances to provide for every aspect of our lives. It requires surrender rather than mere acceptance—a deliberate space for His miraculous work.

By embracing a mindset rooted in the kingdom and prioritizing our relationship with God above all else, we open ourselves up to a current of abundance that surpasses our earthly wants. Let us embark on this journey with unwavering faith, knowing God's unwavering loyalty will accompany us through every trial and triumph. As a Christian author, Max Lucado beautifully expresses, "When we trust in God's loyalty, we will experience a life of overflowing blessings and abundance beyond our wildest dreams."

A bounty far beyond material wealth.

In the scheme of things, when it comes to the provision from the kingdom of God, no one is left lacking. Putting our trust in God's loyalty reveals a bounty far beyond material wealth—nourishing the soul and bringing enlightenment. Throughout history, countless individuals have experienced this truth first-hand. Have been compelled to share their personal stories, allowing others to witness the transformative power of God's provision.

This message deeply resonates with us as it speaks to our desire for fulfilment and contentment. We often mistakenly seek material riches and possessions, believing that they will satisfy the longings of our hearts.

Another author who explores this subject is Max Lucado in his thought-provoking book titled "Less Fret, Faith." Lucado reminds us to release our worries and anxieties with faith in God and His commitment. In the plan of Kingdom Provision, we can rest assured that our needs will be met and our spirits will be nourished. He shares stories of individuals who faced insurmountable challenges but discovered peace and provision through their steadfast faith.

Lucado's message serves as a reminder for us to pause and reflect on our own lives. How often do we? Agonize about the future, allowing thoughts of scarcity and inadequacy to consume us? We must remember that God's provision encompasses more than just material wealth. It includes the provision of love, joy, peace and all the virtues of the Spirit.

When we align our hearts and minds with His will, we tap into an abundant source that surpasses earthly desires. Inspiration can also be found in Sheila Walsh's words in her book "God Has a Dream for Your Life." Walsh beautifully conveys that placing trust in God's faithfulness brings enlightenment to the soul. In her exploration, she delves into how God envisions dreams and desires for everyone, assuring us that He has a purpose and plan for our lives. When we surrender ourselves to His guidance, we discover a sense of fulfilment and direction. Walsh's book is a treasure trove of wisdom, drawing from her own personal experiences as well as the stories of others. She encourages her readers to embrace their unique qualities and believe God's provision will lead them to discover their true calling. With every page turned, Walsh invites us to open our hearts to the abundance and fulfilment that arises from relying on God's faithfulness.

Embracing and trusting in the concept of Kingdom Provision brings about transformative enlightenment. It reminds us that no one is left lacking in the grand scheme of things within God's faithfulness. Through this trust, we uncover blessings beyond material wealth – our hearts are nourished, and our souls are enlightened.

Profound nourishment and provisions.

Like when we plant a seed with faith, we will experience the abundant blessings of God's grace. Trusting in His faithfulness leads to His Kingdom's profound nourishment and provisions. This beautiful truth is interwoven throughout the fabric of the Christian belief system, echoing the promises documented in the

Holy Scriptures. In this journey, we will explore our faith. Uncover the depths of God's faithfulness, His unchanging love, and the abundance that comes from wholeheartedly relying on Him.

Our expedition commences with the words spoken by Jesus in Matthew 6:33, where He encourages His followers to prioritize seeking God's kingdom and righteousness above all else. By doing so, we unlock a floodgate of divine provision that pours into our lives. It is an invitation to release our worries and fears while embracing the assurance that God's faithfulness never wavers.

As we delve deeper into this truth, let us ponder the impactful words of Paul—the apostle whose teachings resonate within our souls.

The book of Philippians 4:19 writes, "And my faith assures me that God will fulfil all your needs according to His blessings in Christ Jesus." This verse beautifully captures the essence of trusting in God's faithfulness. Our heavenly Father, who holds the entirety of the universe within His loving hands, promises to take care of our needs. All we need to do is trust Him and rely on His abundant provision.

Throughout history, there have been stories and accounts of individuals who have witnessed first-hand the fulfilment of this promise. One such example is the story of Elijah and the widow from Zarephath, as depicted in the Bible. Despite being faced with circumstances during a famine, they were miraculously sustained by just a tiny jar filled with oil and a handful of flour. Similarly, there are tales shared by missionaries who have experienced God's unwavering faithfulness in even the world's most remote corners. These narratives serve as testimonies to highlight how putting our trust in God's provision can truly work wonders.

Take, for instance, Hudson Taylor, a Christian author and missionary whose life story exemplifies how limitless God's provision can be. In his memoir "A Retrospect ", he recounts his journey to China and recalls facing numerous challenges and obstacles. However, during each season marked by need or difficulty, he witnessed first-hand how God faithfully provided for him and his mission through unexpected means. His life stands as a testament to the rewards that arise from placing trust in the faithfulness of God.

Furthermore, the writings of C.S. Lewis provide insights into the idea of Kingdom Provision. In his book "Mere Christianity ", he affirms, "God cannot grant us happiness and peace outside of Himself simply because it does not exist independently. There is nothing." Lewis reminds us that genuine nourishment and fulfilment can only be discovered in God. When we have faith in His faithfulness, we tap into the resources offered by His Kingdom. We find the profound satisfaction and contentment our souls yearn for through Him.

As we remain grounded in faith and trust God's faithfulness, we open ourselves to experience the sustenance provided by Kingdom Provision. The Bible, along with Christian author's testimonies, attests to the transformative power of this truth. Let us be inspired and encouraged by this truth to walk with unwavering faith, knowing that when we put our trust in God's faithfulness, we will receive blessings from His Kingdom.

God's infinite love meets our needs.

God's limitless love for humanity knows no bounds. He continuously provides for our needs even before we become conscious of them. The concept of Kingdom Provision stands as evidence of His faithfulness and eternal care for our lives.

In a world filled with uncertainties and challenges, Ann Voskamp beautifully explores the depth of God's provision in her selling book "One Thousand Gifts." Drawing from her personal experiences, Ann shares stories where God's faithful love remained steadfast even during the darkest moments. Her narrative reminds us that when we trust God's goodness, we can discover joy in every circumstance while recognizing His provisions in significant and small ways.

In the book titled "The Circle Maker " written by Mark Batterson, he delves into the idea of prayers and their connection to God's abundant provision. Batterson encourages readers to approach God with unwavering faith, believing He will meet our needs according to His plan. He beautifully intertwines stories of condition with biblical principles, reminding us that persistent prayer and steadfast trust awaken God's provision.

Taking inspiration from Max Lucado's book "It's Not About Me ", we are reminded that God's provision goes beyond our needs. Lucado gently urges us to develop a heart understanding that as we prioritize the needs of others, God will also take care of our own needs. His narrative emphasizes that God's provision is not about fulfilling our earthly desires but rather about the transformative power of love and compassion.

Through his account in "End of the Spear ", Steve Saint explores the remarkable testimony of God's provision in the face of unimaginable challenges. Through his Father's martyrdom as a missionary Saint, he demonstrates that God's condition is not always immediately visible but is often fulfilled through a purpose in our lives.

The story of Saint motivates us to have faith in God's plan, understanding that when faced with challenges, He will provide for us in ways that surpass our comprehension.

In the realm of God's provision, we embrace the truth that His limitless love meets our needs even before we realize them. As we recognize His provision with gratitude in our hearts, the Kingdom of God is magnified, motivating us to be conduits of His condition in the lives of others.

A spiritual abundance that surpasses earthly lack.

Individuals in a world consumed by desires need to redirect their hopes and aspirations towards the unwavering faithfulness of God. By aligning our hearts with His plan, we open ourselves to receiving an abundance, surpassing any lack we may experience on Earth. This abundance goes beyond material possessions. Brings about a profound transformation within us.

In Rick Warrens's book "The Purpose Driven Life ", he reminds us that our true purpose lies in living according to God's will. When we anchor our hopes in His faithfulness, we align ourselves with His purpose. We realize that pursuing possessions and recognition leads to emptiness and transience. Instead, we shift our focus to Kingdom Provision—an abundance that infiltrates every aspect of our existence. Warren eloquently states, "When God grants you a vision, He also equips you with what you need to pursue it."

Drawing inspiration from the writings of Sarah Young in her book "Jesus Calling ", we are encouraged to find comfort, strength and hope in the presence of God. When we trust Him, we acknowledge His faithfulness to fulfil all our needs. By surrendering our worries, doubts, and fears to Him, we make room for His peace and provision to fill our lives. Young reminds us that when we seek His face, put our hope in Him, and trust His faithfulness, we will discover the abundance and fulfilment that only He can provide.

In "Anxious for Nothing ", Max Lucado emphasizes that our hope should not be rooted in things but rather in God's unfailing faithfulness that surpasses any lack or scarcity on Earth. He challenges us to shift our perspective from scarcity to abundance and trust God's provision during difficult times. Lucado says we can replace anxiety with trust by saturating our thoughts with God's faithfulness. Experience a peace that surpasses all understanding.

To deepen our understanding of Kingdom Provision, let us turn to the wisdom of C.S. Lewis as expressed in his book "Mere Christianity." Lewis prompts us to recognize that God's provision goes beyond material needs; it encompasses more than just physical possessions or resources. When we entirely rely on God's faithfulness, our lives are filled with abundant blessings, such as love, joy, peace, and purpose. Every aspect of our existence, including our relationships and daily pursuits, becomes a testament to the faithfulness of God. As C.S. Lewis once said,

God grants us what we truly need rather than simply fulfilling what we may think we want.

As we journey through life, we must acknowledge that genuine abundance can be found in placing our hopes in God's faithfulness. By aligning our desires with His plan, we open ourselves up to experience the transformative power of His provision for His Kingdom. Through this surrendering process, we discover an abundance that far surpasses any earthly lack.

Boundless love under His Divine guidance.

Let us delve into the concept of Kingdom Provision and how wholeheartedly trusting in God's faithfulness can lead us to experience care, affectionate, cherished, and boundless love under His Divine guidance. We will explore the profound love of God and discover how it can transform our lives when we place our trust in Him.

At the core of Kingdom Provision lies the understanding that God is not just a provider but also a caretaker. As we embark on this journey, let us reflect on the beautiful words of C.S. Lewis; "Though we may choose to ignore it, we cannot escape God's presence. He permeates every corner of the world, walking among us incognito." This truth reminds us that God's care and provision are always with us, intricately woven into every aspect of our existence. Regardless of our circumstances, we can find comfort in knowing that He keeps a watchful eye over us.

To truly experience the blessings of Kingdom Provision, we must first place unwavering trust in God's faithfulness. A.W. Tozer expressed this sentiment eloquently when he said, "Whatever I am is because of who God is and whatever He possesses is mine as well." This powerful statement highlights that we align ourselves with His divine plan for our lives by acknowledging God's faithfulness. Such trust requires letting go of doubt and fear while recognizing that His provision surpasses comprehension. We open ourselves to receiving His blessings and transformative power as we trust His faithfulness.

Kingdom Provision encompasses God's providence, tender care, and nurturing. In Psalm 23:1, David proclaims, "The Lord is my shepherd; I lack nothing." This beautiful comparison portrays God as our loving guide leading us through life's ups and downs. Like a shepherd diligently watches over and takes care of each sheep, our Heavenly Father tenderly looks after us with deep respect and affection.

At the heart of Kingdom Provision lies the truth of God's boundless love. Brennan Manning poignantly reminds us to "Embrace your identity as someone deeply loved by God. This is your essence ", highlighting the incomprehensible love and acceptance from God. When we truly grasp the extent of God's love for us, we can let go of insecurities, shame and doubts that burden us. Under His watchful eye, we discover a safe refuge where we are treasured and surrounded by His unwavering love. Through His love for us, He beckons us to live a life filled with joy and the assurance of an eternity spent with Him.

In this part of the book, we have delved into the idea of Kingdom Provision having faith in God's faithfulness. When we embrace this truth and fully surrender ourselves to His guidance, we can find comfort in His constant presence and enjoy the richness of a life lived under the blessings of Kingdom Provision. May this story. Motivate us to cultivate unwavering trust in God and appreciate the abundant benefits that come from His faithful nature.

Chapter Nine

In His Kingdom Purpose

Uncovering and Fulfilling God's Unique Plan

In the fabric of our existence, each person possesses a distinct purpose intricately woven by the Master Creator Himself. At the core of this purpose lies a truth: we are all summoned to fulfil a higher calling and play an essential role in God's grand narrative. Once discovered and embraced, this sacred calling can lead to a life filled with fulfilment, influence, and everlasting significance. Within the pages of this chapter, Uncovering and Fulfilling God's Unique Plan, we embark on a voyage of self-discovery, seeking to comprehend the depths of our callings and how to live them out with passion and unwavering faith courageously.

To truly grasp the essence of our calling, we must delve into sacred scriptures while drawing wisdom from esteemed Bible scholars and Christian authors. As Matthew Henry eloquently expressed in his commentary from the 17th century, "Humanity exists for the glory of God; only by living in alignment with this purpose can one truly find fulfilment" (Henry, 1864).

Our purpose is to align our desires, talents and actions with the will and glory of our Heavenly Father.

According to God's Word, each one of us is lovely. Designed with intricate detail for a specific role in advancing His Kingdom. In his letter to the Romans, the apostle Paul emphasizes the diversity within the body of Christ by saying, "Just as a body has parts but all its many parts form one body, so it is with Christ" (Romans 12:4-5 ESV). Our callings are like puzzle pieces that fit together beautifully, demonstrating God's love and grace.

To discover our God-given calling, we must embark on a journey of self-discovery. Remain open to the leading of the Holy Spirit. As expressed by Christian author Os Guinness, "Calling is the truth that God calls us to Himself in such a way that everything about us – who we are, what we do and what we have – becomes invested with special devotion and dynamism as we respond to His summons, for service" (Guinness, 1998). Through moments of stillness within our hearts and deep contemplation, we can uncover how God intends to utilize our talents, passions, and life experiences to impact the world positively.

Discovering and fulfilling our purpose within God's Kingdom requires a leap of faith, often calling for us to step outside our comfort zones and let go of control. As the esteemed theologian and scholar C.S. Lewis once expressed, "The remarkable thing is when one ceases to view unpleasant events as interruptions to their 'own' or 'real' existence. In truth, what we label as interruptions are indeed the essence of our lives" (Lewis, 1955). Our journey towards fulfilling our purpose may present challenges and unexpected paths. Yet, they serve as opportunities for personal growth and reliance on God's guidance and strength.

Uncovering and Fulfilling God's Unique Plan invites readers on an expedition of self-discovery, faithfulness, and surrender. Drawing wisdom from scholars, renowned authors and the timeless truths found in God's Word, this book strives to inspire individuals to embrace their unique calling wholeheartedly while ushering forth God's Kingdom throughout all aspects of life.

Let us take to heart the words of the Psalmist who proclaimed, "I call upon God Most High, who fulfils his plan for me" (Psalm 57:2 ESV) and may our hearts align with the harmony of our Kingdom Purpose as we carry out the callings entrusted to us.

I am the Conductor. Every symphony has its designated notes.

As I closed my eyes. Let myself be carried away by a sense of surrender, a gentle voice whispered within me. It was a voice filled with wisdom and a touch of humour. *"You See "* it said, *"this is quite similar to my kingdom. I am the Conductor. Every symphony has its designated notes."*

One morning, as the sun began to rise and painted the sky with hues of pink and orange, I found myself settling into my spot for my morning moments of reflection. With a heart seeking guidance and inspiration, I opened my Bible. Started reading. Little did I realize that within those pages lay a tale that would unfold before me, leading me to a profound moment of realization and connection with God.

Lost in the depths of my devotions, a gentle melody softly played in the background. Intrigued by its captivating tune, I paused to immerse myself in the music, not wanting to miss even a single note. It was a worship song called "Lilim" by Victory Worship Philippines, sung in the Tagalog language. From the first moment that its harmonious melodies reached my ears, I sensed that something extraordinary was about to transpire.

The song wrapped around me like an embrace—a soothing balm for my soul—. Filled me with wonderment. The lyrics of this song deeply resonated with me, serving as a reminder of God's love and faithfulness. With each verse and chorus, it felt as if His presence drew closer as if He used this music to touch the essence of my being.

However, what truly captivated me was not just the lyrics themselves. How all the instruments seamlessly blended to create a symphony that emanated harmony. The piano flowed like rain, the guitars were strummed with precision and tenderness, and the drums provided a steady heartbeat. It felt as though they were weaving a masterpiece of artistry.

As I closed my eyes and surrendered myself to God's embrace, I heard a whisper in the depths of my soul. It was a voice filled with wisdom and a touch of humour. *"You see "*, it gently spoke, *"this is quite similar to my kingdom. I am the Conductor, and every symphony must play their designated notes."*

That moment became an epiphany for me—a glimpse into the purpose and beauty found in the diversity within the body of Christ. Just as each instrument has its role in creating a symphony, every individual has a unique part to play in this magnificent orchestration we call life. No position is insignificant because every person's contribution adds to God's awe-inspiring composition.

I discovered a deep appreciation for my purpose in God's kingdom in that revelation. Whether I take the stage with a leading melody or offer support, I realize that each note I play can bring glory to Him.

I am unique, intricately crafted, and perfectly positioned to fulfil a purpose specifically designed for me.

This realization became a guiding light as I entered the world that day. Inspired by the lyrics of "Lilim" and its shared wisdom, I intended to embrace my calling and live a life honouring God in all aspects. Understanding my place within God's kingdom compelled me to inspire others to uncover their purpose and wholeheartedly embrace it.

As the song lyrics of "Lilim" touch the body of Christ as it has touched me. May the heavenly whisper I encountered that morning serve as a source of inspiration for you, too. Like a symphony comes alive through harmonizing every instrument, each person has an important role. Embrace your gifts, talents and calling confidently, knowing that God—the Conductor—will lovingly guide you to perform your part excellently.

God, The Maestro of Your Symphony.

In the symphony of life, it is expected to feel overwhelmed amidst the tunes of uncertainty and confusion. However, amidst this discordance, there exists a conductor who meticulously orchestrates every intricate aspect of our existence. God assumes the role of Conductor in our symphony; with His guiding baton, He leads us towards our purpose and calling. Through His wisdom and boundless grace, we discover, fulfil, and enhance our talents to produce resounding notes that reverberate throughout life's grand orchestra.

As people of faith, we are summoned to embrace our purposes within this world and utilize the unique gifts bestowed upon us by God for His glory. Just as a conductor thoughtfully selects each instrument in an orchestra, God has intricately designed each of us with a purpose. The beauty of Psalm 139:13-16 lies in David's words, where he expresses gratitude for how God formed him in his mother's womb. The intricacy of God's creation and the extraordinary nature of our existence are acknowledged with praise. David recognizes that even before his physical form was visible, God saw every detail and had a plan for his life written in His book.

This revelation serves as a reminder that each of us is uniquely designed by God, equipped with talents and abilities to fulfil our divine purpose. Like the harmonious blend of various instruments in a symphony, our contributions are vital to the overall composition of life. As Max Lucado wisely puts it, "Your talents serve a purpose, then just personal gain; they allow you to make a meaningful impact." Our calling extends beyond personal success or achievements; it is intricately intertwined with God's global plan.

However, discovering and embracing our calling can often appear overwhelming. We may question our capabilities. Struggle with feelings of inadequacy.

The Bible assures us that God equips us with everything to fulfil our purpose. In the book of Exodus, when God called upon Moses to lead the Israelites out of

Egypt, Moses questioned his capability by saying, "Who am I to go to Pharaoh and free the Israelites from Egypt?" (Exodus 3:11). God reassured Moses by affirming, "I will be there with you" (Exodus 3:12). This meaningful interaction serves as a reminder that our worthiness and abilities are not based on our strength alone but on God's presence and guidance in our lives.

As we embrace our calling, we are tasked with utilizing and magnifying our unique gifts and talents for the glory of God. Christian writer John Piper beautifully expresses this concept: "God is most glorified in us when we find satisfaction in Him." When we wholeheartedly dedicate our talents and abilities to serve God's purpose, our lives become a melody of worship and praise. Our gifts are not meant to be concealed; they are intended to be shared with the world to bring hope, joy, and transformation.

God, the Conductor of our life symphony – invites us to discover, fulfil and amplify our calling within the grand orchestra of life. Through the wisdom and blessings bestowed upon us, we are intricately fashioned with talents and capabilities to contribute to the great plan set by a higher power. Let us answer the call, embrace our purpose, and rely on guidance as we fulfil our unique calling. As renowned Christian authors like Max Lucado, John Piper and many others have imparted through their teachings, our talents are not meant for gain alone but to make a meaningful impact. May our lives harmonize like a symphony of worship and praise resonating with melodies that bring honour to the one who orchestrates our souls.

An opportunity to unveil the masterpiece you were destined to become.

Finding solace and purpose in God's blueprint for our lives is a blessing in a world often marred by chaos and uncertainty. Embracing each day as an occasion for growth. Revealing the magnificent creation, we were intended to be calls for unwavering faith, hopefulness, and an unyielding commitment to selfless service in His Kingdom.

In his book " For Nothing, " Max Lucado, a Christian author, beautifully captures the essence of approaching each day as an opportunity. He reminds us that no matter our challenges, God has a plan for our lives that surpasses our comprehension. When we embrace each day with faith and surrender, we allow God to reveal His purpose within us. This requires a mindset that values gratitude because it is through gratefulness that we discover the strength to move forward and embrace the responsibilities entrusted to us by God.

God's blueprint for our lives is like a masterpiece—a creation filled with love and purpose. As John Eldredge, a theologian, profoundly expresses in his book "Wild at Heart ", God has endowed us with unique gifts, talents and passions that reflect His image. To unveil the work within us, we must find the courage to embrace our true selves and live out our divine calling. It is through vulnerability. Letting go of societal expectations that we can genuinely radiate with authenticity. We are tasked with being a source of hope, a guiding light in times of darkness, revealing the power of God's love. In his book "The Purpose Driven Life ", Christian writer Rick Warren encourages us to see our lives as a mission field, reminding us that we were created with a purpose other than our desires. By radiating love, compassion, and support, we become beacons of hope for those who may have lost their way. Through our actions and love for others, we fulfil our purpose of being a beacon of hope.

The path to embracing our purpose involves acts of service. Drawing inspiration from the teachings of Mother Teresa, Christian author Richard J. Foster highlights the transformative power of serving others in his book "Celebration of Discipline." By putting aside our desires and ego, we find strength in humility and become vessels through which God's love flows. When we serve others, we honour God's calling. Fulfil our purpose by providing comfort and support to those we encounter along our journey.

While discovering our purpose, we must remember that we are children of God called to serve, inspire, and bring hope to a world in need.

The Church is a symphony that allows us to embrace the enchanting melody.

Within the symphony of life composition, the Church and community hold positions similar to well-tuned instruments within a harmonious orchestra. They blend unity, love, and comprehension, forming a symphony that allows us to embrace the enchanting melody of our Divine Calling. The Church, empowered by God's wisdom, offers guidance and support as we navigate life's journey.

In His wisdom, God has brought together individuals from diverse backgrounds, cultures, and life experiences to establish the body of Christ. The Church. As stated in 1 Corinthians 12:27, "Now you are the body of Christ and individually members of it." Each person within the Church plays a role akin to various instruments in an orchestra. Some may possess qualities like brass instruments, while others embody a gentle spirit similar to flutes. However, when we unite under God's guidance and word, we create a symphony that resonates with messages of love and understanding.

Timothy Keller, an author known for his book "The Meaning of Marriage ", beautifully explains how the Church and community are interconnected with our purpose. In his words, "The Church is like God inviting all these people mismatched and flawed to join Him at a banquet. Here's some wine, for you. "Keller emphasizes that the Church goes beyond being a physical structure or an organization; it is a thriving community where imperfect individuals can find comfort, support and forgiveness. It serves as a nurturing space for growth and spiritual development, offering the valuable support of fellow believers.

When we immerse ourselves in a community of minded individuals who share our beliefs, we open ourselves up to opportunities for learning, personal development and being part of something greater than ourselves. Similar to how plants require soil and nourishing sunlight to flourish, we, too, need a positive and supportive environment to thrive in fulfilling our purpose. The Church provides an environment—a community that empowers us to embrace our unique calling within the kingdom.

Rick Warren, another known Christian author who wrote "The Purpose Driven Life", encourages us to actively engage with our community and utilize the talents bestowed upon us by God for serving others. He emphasizes that we have gifts, opportunities, and abilities to make a meaningful difference. Our purpose extends beyond individual accomplishments or ambitions; it revolves around positively impacting the lives of those around us.

When we actively involve ourselves in our community by serving and showing love, we open the door for God's intervention and guidance. By embracing our purpose within the kingdom and utilizing our talents for the betterment of others, we become channels through which God's love and grace flow to those around us. As we selflessly dedicate ourselves to serving others, we become real-life examples of how God's transformative power can impact lives, motivating others to seek a connection with Him.

When the Church and community operate as they should, they embody the artistry of God. They work together like instruments in a symphony that produces harmony, love and understanding. Through participation in the Church, we find the motivation, assistance, and wisdom necessary to fulfil our purpose and leave a lasting positive influence on the world.

Church and community hold roles within God's grand life design. They harmonize unity, love and understanding while assisting us in embracing our Kingdom Purpose. By engaging with fellow believers in a communal setting and utilizing our gifts for good causes, we become vessels of God's affectionate care and grace—inspiring others to embrace their divine purpose.

Let's draw inspiration from Christian authors like Timothy Keller and Rick Warren as they emphasize the significance of community and its transformative potential when we wholeheartedly embrace God's plan. Together, let us embody our purpose, guided by the symphony orchestrated by the Church and our surrounding community.

Inspiration is boundless and everlasting.

In this fast-paced and ever-changing world, it can be easy to lose sight of our purpose sometimes. We become engrossed in pursuing success, wealth and material possessions while forgetting that life holds a deeper meaning. As followers of Christ, we are called to a purpose. This purpose surpasses our individual lives and influences the world around us. This purpose is often referred to as our Kingdom Purpose, which is uniquely designed for each one of us by God. We experience a life filled with fulfilment, meaning, and positive influence when we embrace this calling.

Discovering and fulfilling our purpose can be likened to dropping a stone into a serene pond. Initially, the stone creates an insignificant splash, but as the ripples travel outward, their influence grows more significant and impactful. Likewise, when we live out our Kingdom Purpose, the waves of love, transformation, and inspiration we generate have enduring effects.

Embarking to uncover and embrace our Kingdom's Purpose is not always a path. It often entails introspection, seeking divine guidance, and stepping beyond our comfort zones. Nevertheless, it is a voyage undertaking because when we align our lives with God's intended purpose, we find a profound sense of fulfilment and genuine happiness that cannot be discovered elsewhere.

The remarkable power of living by our Kingdom Purpose is beautifully exemplified in the stories of biblical figures. Consider Joseph's narrative as an illustration. Despite enduring years of betrayal, enslavement and imprisonment, Joseph remained steadfast in his faithfulness to God while pursuing his mission of saving his people. Through unwavering devotion and perseverance, he rescued Egypt from calamity. He brought about love-filled reconciliation within his family—a ripple effect reverberating for generations.

Esther's story is truly inspiring. Despite being an orphan and a young Jewish woman, she faced challenges and obstacles with great courage. She embraced her purpose. Fearlessly stepped into her calling to rescue her people from utter destruction. Esther's bravery and unwavering trust in God saved her people. They made her a symbol of courage and faith for generations to come.

These tales from the Bible remind us that when we live out our purpose, even in the face of adversity, we can leave a lasting impact on the world around us. They encourage us to pursue our goals, knowing that God is always by our side, guiding and empowering us.

Living out our purpose also entails leading a life of love and service. As followers of Christ, we are called to love our neighbours and extend love towards our enemies. Through acts of love and compassion, we can transform the world. We can draw inspiration from Jesus' life, who selflessly loved and served others, going as far as sacrificing his own life for humanity's sake.

Recognizing and embracing our purpose given by a higher power is a genuinely transformative calling with the potential to shape the world and leave behind a lasting legacy of love and inspiration. Achieving our purpose involves introspection, seeking divine guidance, and courage to take leaps of faith. The rewards are priceless as we find fulfilment and genuine happiness that cannot be obtained solely through wealth and success. As we embark on this journey, let us find inspiration from the individuals mentioned in narratives who wholeheartedly embraced their purpose and made an enduring impact on the world. May we strive to love, serve, and live our lives so that our acts of kindness, positive change and motivational influence continue spreading for future generations.

Chapter Ten

In His Kingdom Transformation

Growing and Maturing in the Likeness of Christ

In our pursuit of growth and transformation, believers all over the globe embark on a lifelong journey to become more like Christ. The Kingdom Transformation idea encompasses maturing and attaining Christlikeness, where we are shaped and moulded by God's love, grace, and wisdom. This book delves into this transformative journey, providing an inspiring story filled with divine wisdom.

As Christians, we aim to reflect the character and nature of Jesus Christ, our Lord and Saviour. The apostle Paul captured the essence of this transformation when he proclaimed, "I have been crucified with Christ; it is no longer I who live, but Christ lives in me" (Galatians 2:20). This transformation goes beyond surface-level changes; it involves a surrender of our old selves to embrace the new life that God offers us through His Son. Kingdom Transformation encompasses a renewal of our souls, a change in our thinking patterns and a reshaping of our hearts so that we can embody Jesus' love, compassion, and righteousness in front of others.

To begin this journey, it's crucial to grasp the foundations that form the basis of Kingdom Transformation. Delving into scripture, we uncover the teachings of Bible scholars like J.I. Packer, who emphasize the significance of fostering a deep connection with God through prayer, contemplation, and a genuine longing to understand His Word. Through this practice, our hearts and minds undergo a profound change as we align our desires with God and equip ourselves to confront both challenges and opportunities that come our way.

Christian writers such as Watchman Nee also guide us in comprehending the Holy Spirit's power in our journey. Nee emphasizes relying on the Spirit's guidance and sheds light on practical aspects of Kingdom Transformation, offering valuable insights and encouragement for our everyday walk with Christ.

Inspired by 2 Corinthians 3:18, which states, "And we all...are being transformed into his image with increasing glory," we are reminded that Kingdom Transformation is an ongoing process. It isn't a destination we reach; instead, it's a pursuit filled with awe-inspiring experiences and divine revelations.

Initiating a journey of kingdom transformation begins by adopting a mindset that mirrors the character of Christ. Through the Holy Spirit's empowerment, we are brought face to face with the awe-inspiring splendour of our Heavenly Father. Aspire to radiate His magnificence as His cherished children.

We realize that God's ways transcend our own, and His wisdom surpasses human comprehension. Christian writers like C.S. Lewis and A.W. Tozer delve into this wisdom, offering profound insights into the enigmatic dimensions of God's love, grace and divine purposes. Their teachings uplift and fortify our faith, shaping how we perceive the voyage ahead.

Growing and maturing in Christlikeness enlightens us on becoming more like Christ while inspiring readers to pursue a deeper connection with God. This book empowers believers to embrace God's transformative love and grace, guiding them towards divine discernment and enabling them to reflect Jesus Christ's glorious image. May this book serve as an instrument of encouragement, inspiration, and spiritual development for believers as they embark on their journey toward kingdom transformation.

Kingdom transformation requires adopting a mindset to that of Christ.

In a world filled with turmoil, it is essential to embark on a journey of growth and transformation. This process begins by cultivating a mindset that reflects the qualities of Christ, allowing us to develop and mature like branches connected to a vine. As we embody His characteristics, our lives serve as a testament to wisdom, inspiring and uplifting those around us.

Kingdom transformation goes beyond surface-level changes or temporary emotional experiences. It entails an inner shift when we willingly surrender ourselves to the transformative work of the Holy Spirit in our lives. We consciously adopt a mindset that mirrors His example by aligning our thoughts, desires, and actions with Christ's teachings. This mindset becomes the driving force behind our growth and transformation. As Dallas Willard eloquently expresses, "Transformation is an ongoing process where we become more like Christ for the sake of others."

As branches intimately connected to the vine, our progress and maturity depend on our willingness to relinquish control and trust in our Heavenly Gardener's guidance.

Like a branch cannot produce fruit independently, we also need nourishment and guidance from Christ to thrive. Henri Nouwen beautifully captures this truth: "The branch that remains connected to the vine doesn't grow bananas; it grows grapes. And it doesn't worry, struggle or strive; it simply grows because of its connection."

The aim of transforming the Kingdom is to embody the likeness of Christ. This means reflecting His nature, character, and love in our lives. As John Ortberg eloquently expresses, "Pursuing a Christ character is not an optional accessory in the Christian life; it's at the core of it." Our thoughts, words and actions should mirror Jesus' unconditional love and grace.

Having a mindset aligned with Christ leads to wisdom. When we surrender ourselves to God's will, our perspective shifts and we gain insights beyond human understanding. James writes, "If any of you lacks wisdom, ask God who gives generously without finding fault, and you will receive it." By seeking guidance from God and allowing His wisdom to influence our decisions and actions, we become channels through which His divine wisdom flows. A.W. Tozer once said, "Wisdom among things involves the ability to envision perfect outcomes and achieve those outcomes using the most ideal methods."

Kingdom transformation begins with nurturing a mindset that resembles Christ's as we do. Grow as branches connected to the Divine Vine; our lives mirror and embody His likeness. This transformation empowers us to inspire and uplift others by living out wisdom.

This transformative journey impacts our lives and enables us to bear fruit that brings glory to God and blesses those around us. Let us strive to be vessels of transformation by renewing our minds to align with the mind of Christ, becoming living examples of His divine love and grace.

The vision for change stems from the privilege of reflecting Christ's image.

The concept of transformation holds great significance and has been extensively explored by notable scholars and authors in Christian literature throughout history. It is deeply rooted in our position as followers of Christ, where we aim to reflect His divine image. As we allow ourselves to be led by the Holy Spirit, we transcend the realm of survival and embark on a transformative journey filled with purpose, illuminating paths for others while nurturing qualities that align with the character of Christ.

Reflecting Christ's image is a theme in the New Testament. In Paul's letter to the Romans, he writes, "And we all who with faces contemplate the Lord's glory are being transformed into his image with ever-increasing glory, which comes from the Lord who is the Spirit" (2 Corinthians 3:18, NIV). This verse emphasizes a process of transformation that takes place as we behold God's glorious presence. This profound change occurs through the work of the Holy Spirit within us as we dedicate ourselves to deepening our understanding of Christ's identity and what His character reveals to us.

The journey towards transformation commences when we consciously surrender ourselves to follow where the Holy Spirit leads us.

When we surrender ourselves, we open to the power of God's grace. According to the known theologian J.I. Packer in his book "Knowing God," being loved and cared for by God the Father is even greater than being right with Him as a judge (Packer, 1993). When we allow the Holy Spirit to guide us, we experience forgiveness for our sins and receive the fullness of God's love, mercy, and grace.

Our lives testify to God's work within us. We start living with a purpose-driven by a desire to reflect Christ's character in our thoughts, words, and actions. In her book "Celebration of Discipline" Richard J. Foster states that what is truly needed today is not more intelligent or gifted individuals but those deep in their understanding (Foster, 1978). Spiritual transformation goes beyond intelligence or talent; it reaches the very core of who we are and enables us to live authentic and honest lives.

Naturally, we find ourselves illuminating paths for others due to our transformation. As we progress in our journey to become more like Christ, our lives shine as beacons of hope in a world filled with darkness. In his book titled "The Divine Conspiracy ", Dallas Willard highlights the importance of this path by stating that it's not merely about believing certain things about God but rather about embodying the qualities of a loving creator and sustainer of life (Willard, 1998) by displaying God's love, compassion and forgiveness, we. Guide others on their own transformative journeys and help them experience the abundant life that Christ offers.

Nurturing Christlike characteristics requires practice and a constant reliance on the guidance of the Holy Spirit. It necessitates committing ourselves to growth and being willing to surrender our own desires and ambitions to God. Brennan Manning beautifully captures the essence of this journey in his book "Abbas Child" when he writes that our true identity lies in recognizing ourselves as deeply loved by God; any other identity is merely an illusion (Manning, 2002). When we genuinely comprehend and embrace God's love for us, it alters how we perceive ourselves and the world around us.

The vision of transformation is an awe-inspiring concept that invites us to reflect on the image of Christ while being led by the Holy Spirit. It is a voyage from existing to living with intention, shedding light on paths and nurturing qualities that resemble Christ. When we surrender ourselves to the power of God's grace, we delve into the profoundness of His love and gain strength to become sources of inspiration and catalysts for positive change in the world. Let us wholeheartedly embrace this vision and consistently strive for growth as we mirror the essence of Christ.

Christlikeness is not a destination. Instead, it is a lifelong journey.

The path of Christlikeness is a transformative journey that unfolds gradually as we walk hand in hand with our Saviour. It is a road filled with both challenges and victories. Every step brings us closer to reflecting the radiant image of Christ. As we wholeheartedly embrace this process, we grow nearer to God and uncover our true identities, purpose, and potential in Him.

In his book "The Journey of Christlikeness ", theologian A.W. Tozer emphasizes that God's ultimate purpose for us is to become more like Jesus. The Holy Spirit works within us, moulding our wills to align with the mind and character of Christ. Tozer's words underscore the core essence of striving for Christlikeness as an aspect of the Christian journey. This deliberate transformation encompasses our hearts, minds, and actions to mirror the very nature of our Lord and Saviour.

Throughout the Bible, individual's lives were profoundly changed through their encounters with Christ. The apostle Paul, who was once hostile towards Christians, had a life-changing encounter with Jesus on the road to Damascus. In one of his letters to the Philippians, Paul writes about his determination to fully grasp what Christ Jesus had taken hold of in him (Philippians 3:12, NIV). Paul's journey towards becoming like Christ was characterized by an unwavering pursuit of knowing and embodying His qualities. This journey demanded perseverance and a willingness to yield to the work of the Holy Spirit.

We must recognize that it is not a fixed destination but an ongoing process. C.S. Lewis, a Christian writer, aptly reminds us in his book "Mere Christianity" that every choice we make can shape us gradually into a heavenly or hellish being. Our choices, actions and attitudes significantly mould our character and determine our path towards Christlikeness.

Every step we take, whether in obedience, love, or forgiveness, brings us closer to reflecting the heart of our Saviour. Through surrender and active pursuit of holiness, we begin to let go of our old selves and embrace the likeness of Christ.

Embracing this process of becoming more like Christ also helps us discover our true identities. The world often pressures us to conform to its standards and expectations, which can lead us away from ourselves in Christ. However, when we align ourselves with God's purpose and strive to embody Jesus' character, we tap into a wellspring of fulfilment and joy.

Becoming like Christ is a continuous journey rather than a destination. It is a pursuit to reflect the heart and character of our Saviour. We are transformed from within, discovering ourselves and finding fulfilment in our close relationship with God. May we find the courage to take each step with hope and faith, knowing that we become like Jesus with every stride.

In our quest to become like Christ, we embark on a transformative journey that extends beyond the limits of time and space. This journey has no destination but offers endless opportunities for growth, insight, and spiritual treasures. Recognizing that becoming Christlike is an ongoing process brings us closer to reflecting His image while also helping us uncover the depths of our authentic selves.

The idea that Christlikeness is a journey rather than a destination reminds us that growing in our faith requires continuous effort and commitment as theologian N.T. Wright beautifully articulates, "The ultimate aim of life is not to escape from this world or our physical bodies but rather to become more like Christ" (Wright, 2016). Conforming to Christ's likeness encompasses every aspect of our existence, influencing our thoughts, words, and actions.

Embracing the divine process of becoming more like Christ is essential to uncover ourselves. This process entails surrendering our desires and allowing God's Spirit to work within us. Christian author Henri Nouwen profoundly encourages us by urging, "Do not hesitate to love... Embrace the pain, without resistance; let your heart be broken, and your tears flow freely" (Nouwen, 1975). By acknowledging the significance of embracing joys and sorrows, we can become more like Christ.

As we walk the path towards Christlikeness, we begin to uncover ourselves. Our identities are reshaped according to His plan as we align ourselves with God's intentions. In his writings, Richard Foster, an author, stresses this truth by stating that "the discovery of who I am lies somehow within the discovery of God" (Foster, 1998). Delving into our relationship with God, we unveil the unique qualities and gifts He has graciously given us. This empowers us to have an impact on the world around us.

We embark on a journey characterized by growth, self-discovery, and transformation. Recognizing that this is a process enables us to approach each day with renewed determination. We know that every step forward brings us closer to reflecting His image. The divine method of embracing Christlikeness invites us to know ourselves and reveal the incredible potential and purpose dwelling within us.

Regard trials as a discipline that fosters growth in faith.

When faced with challenges, it is crucial to perceive them as opportunities for spiritual growth. The winds of change shape our character and enable us to become agents of positive change in society. Although we may desire moments of calmness and tranquillity during life's storms, it is through trials and tribulations that our faith is truly tested and refined. By embracing these hardships as lessons, we shift our perspective from mere suffering to an avenue for personal development and spiritual transformation.

The idea of viewing trials as divine discipline can be found throughout sections of religious texts. For instance, in the book of Hebrews, the author reminds us not to take the Lord's discipline but instead find strength amidst His rebukes because it is through a field that God demonstrates His love for His children (Hebrews 12:5 6 NIV). Therefore, rather than interpreting trials as signs of God's absence or neglect, we should recognize them as expressions of His affectionate guidance that shapes us into reflections of His Son.

The wind holds significance in religious texts, representing the movement of God's Spirit and the potential for transformative change. As physical wind shapes landscapes, the winds of change in our lives can shape us into catalysts for Kingdom Transformation. The book of Isaiah says, "I will make rivers flow on heights and springs within the valleys. I will turn the desert into pools of water. Parched ground into springs" (Isaiah 41:18 NIV). God's transformative power can bring new life and hope in our most barren moments.

Warren W. Wiersbe, a scholar of biblical texts, reminds us that trials provide growth opportunities in character and faith. Approaching problems with a Christ-centred perspective enables advancement. These challenges push us to rely on God's strength and wisdom, deepening our faith and trust in Him. As we lean on Him amidst adversity, we witness His faithfulness. Experience a peace that surpasses all understanding (Philippians 4:7).

A.W. Tozer, a Christian author, encourages us to embrace the refining process by stating that it is through hurt that God can bless someone greatly. This statement serves as a reminder that growth often occurs during times. Our true character is formed through life's struggles, and our faith becomes more robust. Just like a diamond is created under heat and pressure, our faith is honed through the testing we face.

When we perceive trials as an opportunity for guidance, it changes our perspective on suffering. By dwelling on the difficulties, we can focus on the potential for personal growth and transformation from them. By embracing God's refining process, we become vessels for His work in this world, agents of change amidst brokenness. Our trials become chances to radiate God's light and offer hope to those around us.

Trials are not designed to shatter us but to build resilience. When viewed through guidance, we realize that God is actively present during our struggles. The winds of change that shape and mould us can transform us into catalysts for Kingdom Transformation. Through trials, our faith, and our character. Our reliance upon God deepened.

As we navigate the trials and tribulations of life from a Christ-centred perspective, we discover hope, encouragement, and divine wisdom to steer us on our path towards growth and transformation.

It all starts with love and persists with hope.

Every step taken in the direction of Jesus brings about a metamorphosis. It all starts with love and persists with hope. Allows the guidance of the Holy Spirit towards embodying a Christlike existence. The transformation of God's Kingdom isn't distant; it commences within you here and now. These profound insights possess the power to inspire and uplift believers to seek a connection with

Jesus—ultimately leading to personal transformation while radiating His love to others.

To fully grasp the impact of every step toward Jesus, we must acknowledge the significance of love as our starting point. Esteemed biblical scholar John Piper beautifully articulates love as a commandment from God and an embodiment of His essence in his renowned work "Desiring God." We align ourselves with His nature by beginning our journey toward Jesus infused with love. Our love for God and others guides our actions, thoughts, and relationships, creating an atmosphere of compassion, forgiveness, and grace.

However, love alone cannot sustain us during life's challenges and hardships. This is where hope becomes crucial. The Apostle Paul wrote in his letter to the Romans that we can find glory in tribulations because they produce perseverance, which builds character, leading to hope (Romans 5:3-4). Christian writer Charles H. Spurgeon once reflected on this verse by comparing expectancy to a star that shines brightest in the darkness of adversity. Spurgeon reminds us that it is through persevering through trials that our character develops, further deepening our hope in Jesus and His promises.

While love and hope are aspects of our journey towards Jesus, the Holy Spirit empowers us to live a life resembling Christ. The Holy Spirit serves as our guide, counsellor, and advocate, showing us the path to follow. In his book "Mere Christianity" esteemed Christian author C.S. Lewis emphasizes the significance of the Holy Spirit in transforming our lives. He states, "He has an impact on us in ways... However, importantly, He influences us through our own thoughts. Whenever we become arrogant, He makes us feel uneasy... He prompts us to experience shame whenever we contemplate ugliness..." Lewis reminds us that the Holy Spirit's work is not limited to methods but also affects our thinking and behaviour. It convicts us of wrongdoing. Motivates us to pursue righteousness.

As believers, we must understand that Kingdom Transformation is not an abstract concept unrelated to our reality. Instead, it begins within us here and now. Dallas Willard, an author and theologian, explains in his book "The Divine

Conspiracy" that the Kingdom of God exists both as a present reality and a future hope. According to Willard's argument, Jesus initiated the Kingdom during His time on Earth. As His followers, we are called to embody the values, principles, and character of the Kingdom. This understanding should inspire us to reflect Jesus' love, hope and transformative power. As a result of this influence on those around us, we contribute towards establishing the Kingdom of God.

Every step we take towards Jesus has the potential to bring about change. By starting with love, persisting with hope, and allowing the guidance of the Holy Spirit, we can embark on a journey towards living a life that reflects Christ's teachings. This path may have its challenges. It also leads to abundant blessings, unwavering faith in Jesus Christ, and a deepened connection with Him. As we internalize these truths and embrace the power of God's Kingdom within us, we become instruments of His love and grace, making a tangible impact on the world around us. Let us value the wisdom shared by Bible scholars and Christian authors, recognizing the significance of each step taken towards Jesus and embracing a life-altering journey towards drawing closer to our Lord and Saviour.

Chapter Eleven

In His Kingdom Warfare

Standing Strong amidst Spiritual Challenges.

In a world constantly besieged by conflicts, it becomes essential for believers to grasp the principles of engaging in God's Kingdom warfare and equipping themselves for forthcoming battles. The trials we encounter in our lives are not happenstances or mere obstacles to overcome; instead, they are spiritual battles that demand us to stand resolute while clad in the armour of God. As highlighted by the apostle Paul in his letter to the Ephesians, "Our struggle is not against flesh and blood. Against rulers against authorities against cosmic powers over this present darkness against the spiritual forces of evil in the heavenly places" (Ephesians 6:12, NIV).

Participating in God's Kingdom warfare deeply resonates with believers who strive to live fearlessly amidst a fallen world. Throughout our journey, we encounter battles that test our faith, shape our character, and impact our relationship with God. Nevertheless, armed with the wisdom found within scripture, we discover both inspiration and encouragement to persist and emerge victorious.

Revered biblical scholars and authors, within circles, have delved into profound depths of understanding regarding spiritual warfare. They offer insights and practical wisdom that guide us along this intricate path.

C.S. Lewis, a known Christian writer and defender of the faith, once expressed the idea that there is no middle ground in the universe. According to him, every inch of space and every moment in time is claimed by God. Contested by Satan. This serves as a reminder that spiritual conflicts are ongoing, and as believers, we have a responsibility to actively engage in Kingdom Warfare, understanding that our fight serves a greater purpose beyond ourselves.

In his book "The Three Battlegrounds ", Francis Frangipane expands on our battles. He emphasizes the need for a mindset and approach when facing spiritual forces. Frangipane highlights three areas where these battles occur: conquering our own fleshly desires, navigating the challenges posed by the world around us, and engaging with the spiritual realm. By remaining firmly rooted in our faith in Christ and resisting temptations, distractions, and deceptions from our adversary, we can stand firm during these conflicts while witnessing God's triumph manifested in our lives.

Another respected biblical scholar named John Eldredge challenges believers through his book "Waking the Dead" to abandon passivity when engaging in spiritual warfare. Instead, he encourages us to embrace a faith ready for battle. Drawing inspiration from truths, Eldredge reminds us that we are not mere bystanders or observers within the realm of spirituality but active participants in God's divine mission.

He motivates us to step forward with faith, confront the adversary, and reclaim territories taken by the enemy.

Moreover, the Bible serves as a source of wisdom and guidance when navigating the complexities of Kingdom Warfare. In his letter to the Corinthians, the apostle Paul reminds us that "while we live in this world our way of waging war is not like that of the world. The weapons we use are not worldly; on the contrary they have power to demolish strongholds" (2 Corinthians 10:3-4 NIV). This passage emphasizes the power bestowed upon us by God to engage in battle against dark forces through prayer, relying on God's Word and invoking Jesus' authority.

Kingdom Warfare goes beyond physical combat; it entails a spiritual struggle against evil forces. As believers, we must stand firm with God's wisdom, courage, and faith as our armour. By grasping the principles of Kingdom Warfare shared by biblical scholars and Christian authors and delving deeper into scripture, we can discover inspiration, encouragement, and godly wisdom necessary for navigating spiritual battles that come our way.

Our faith acts as an unwavering stronghold.

Amidst the battle for righteousness, our faith acts as an unwavering stronghold, showcasing the depth of our conviction and the incredible power bestowed upon us by God. As believers, we struggle beyond what meets the eye, constantly contending with forces seeking to weaken our faith and undermine our confidence. Our steadfast faith finds its actual strength and purpose during these trying moments. Drawing inspiration from Bible scholars and Christian authors, we aim to delve into the profound message conveyed in this passage and its significance for present-day followers of Christ.

The idea of faith resonates throughout scripture, reminding us that regardless of circumstances, our trust in God must remain unwavering. As distinguished biblical scholar, R.C. Sproul aptly asserts, "Faith is the cornerstone virtue from which all other virtues flow." Our steadfast belief in God serves as a bedrock for navigating the challenges posed by spiritual battles, equipping us to confront adversity head-on.

Within our convictions lies the profound ability to tap into God's divine power. Hebrews 11:1 beautifully captures this truth, expressing faith as the confidence in what we hope for and the assurance of unseen things. We unleash the invisible yet tangible manifestation of God's power from within us by standing amidst challenges and unwaveringly trusting in His promises. As esteemed scholar Oswald Chambers reminds us, faith is not merely believing without evidence. Instead, we place our complete trust in God without reservation.

The concept of kingdom warfare refers to the battle surrounding us, where visible and invisible adversaries are encountered. In his letter to the Ephesians, Apostle Paul encourages believers to "put on the armour of God" (Ephesians 6;11) to courageously confront these unseen forces. Our faith becomes a shield of strength and an unstoppable weapon within this context. It is a refuge amidst chaos, empowering us to resist the enemy's schemes (Ephesians 6:16).

When we truly grasp the depths of our faith, we realize that it relies not solely on our strength but on God's power working within us. Theologian and author A.W. Tozer wisely emphasizes that our thoughts about God significantly shape who we are.

Our belief in God's power and his unwavering Love fuels our faith. He enables us to experience the full extent of His strength.

As we navigate the challenges of battles, we must surround ourselves with insights from God's Word and respected Bible scholars and Christian authors. When we reflect on the writings of individuals such as C.S. Lewis, John Piper, Henri Nouwen, and others, we gain fresh perspectives on the significance of faith and enlightenment during times of spiritual warfare. By immersing ourselves in their works, we equip ourselves with the necessary wisdom to face the trials that lie ahead.

Our faith acts as a fortress amidst the difficulties encountered in spiritual warfare. It showcases our deep-rooted beliefs and reveals God's powerful presence within us. As we continually rely on God's promises and unwavering Love, we become warriors in this spiritual battle—beacons of hope radiating divine power. May our unwavering faith inspire others to seek God's trust in His sustaining power and ultimately experience victory in their spiritual warfare.

It is not one's imagination but a tangible reality that tests life itself.

Embracing the wisdom of God is essential as it provides us peace in times of turmoil and guidance when things seem unclear. It's important to remember that spiritual warfare is not just a concept. A tangible reality that puts our very existence to the test during life's trials and tribulations. In these moments, we are called upon to seek solace in God's peace amidst chaos and rely on His guidance when things seem uncertain. As followers of Christ, we find assurance that victory is already guaranteed when we entrust ourselves to spiritual warfare. We will explore the significance of warfare by delving into the profound wisdom found in the Bible and drawing insights from respected biblical scholars and Christian authors.

When contemplating warfare, it becomes crucial to recognize its importance. The Apostle Paul eloquently expressed this truth; "For our struggle is not against flesh and blood. Against rulers against authorities against cosmic powers over this present darkness against the spiritual forces of evil, in the heavenly places" (Ephesians 6:12 ESV). This verse highlights the reality of warfare beyond what our physical senses can perceive. Spiritual battles are not just theoretical. Real struggles that profoundly impact our lives and test our faith.

In moments of warfare, it becomes crucial to embrace the wisdom of God and find comfort in His peace. Jesus assured us in John 16:33, "I have shared these things with you so that you may experience peace in me. In this world, you will face difficulties. Take courage! I have conquered the world." These words from Christ encourage us to seek solace in His promise of triumph and lasting serenity even when confronted with life's storms.

Amidst warfare, where confusion and ambiguity often reign, we are reminded to seek divine guidance from God. The psalmist proclaims, "Your word is a guiding light, for my steps; it illuminates my path" (Psalm 119:105, NIV). Scripture acts as a beacon that guides us on our journey and imparts heavenly wisdom to navigate through the tumultuous challenges of spiritual warfare. By immersing ourselves in the Word of God, we gain the clarity and discernment necessary to overcome the schemes plotted by the adversary.

As followers of Christ who actively engage in the reality of spiritual warfare, we can find solace in knowing that ultimate victory awaits us. The Apostle Paul, under the guidance of the Holy Spirit, writes in Romans 8:37 (NIV), "No in all these things we are more than conquerors through him who loved us." This powerful statement reminds us that victory isn't a possibility but something already achieved through Jesus Christ. When we trust Him, we gain the strength to face battles confidently, knowing that the fight has already been won.

Spiritual warfare isn't a product of our imagination but a real challenge that tests every aspect of our lives. However, as believers, we can embrace God's wisdom and find His peace amidst chaos. In times of uncertainty, we can seek His guidance by immersing ourselves in the knowledge found within the Bible and drawing from the insights shared by respected Bible scholars and Christian authors. Through these means, we can navigate through. Emerge victorious from the trials of spiritual warfare. Let's find encouragement in God's assurance of victory and face warfare with unwavering faith and determined resolve.

Conquerors rather than defeat. Empowered, rather than lacking power.

In warfare, we stand as conquerors rather than the defeated. We are empowered, rather than lacking power. We triumph and achieve so much more through the Love bestowed upon us. These words resonate deeply with truth and strength, reminding us of the resilience and potential that resides within us on our spiritual journey. We can rise above adversity and overcome life's challenges through God's Love.

One of the comforting aspects of our faith lies in knowing that we are never alone in our struggles. The scriptures assure us that the Lord stands by our side, fighting on our behalf. As stated in Ephesians 6:12, the apostle Paul reminds us that our battle is not against mortals but against rulers, authorities, and powers of Darkness in heavenly realms. This verse reveals the reality of our struggle and the assurance that we need not face it alone. Our ultimate victory rests securely in God's hands.

As Lewis once eloquently wrote, "In times of pleasure, God whispers to us; in moments of conscience, He speaks softly. It is through our painful experiences that He raises His voice like a megaphone to awaken a deaf world." This poignant quote reminds us that even during our most challenging moments, God's Love and strength are always present, ready to uplift and guide us towards triumph.

A Christian author, Max Lucado, echoes similar sentiments in his book "Unshakable Hope: Building Our Lives on the Promises of God." Lucado inspires readers to cling to God's promises during times of hardship. He beautifully expresses this idea by saying, "When engaged in battle it is often the person on the line who faces enemy fire. However, it is, from behind that orders are given. It is God who stands firmly behind us." He has control over everything. This reminder encourages us to stay firm in our faith, understanding that God's Love and authority lead us through every challenge.

The idea of being victorious through Christ's Love is beautifully expressed in the New Testament in Romans 8:37, "No despite all these things overwhelming victory is ours through Christ, who loved us." The words of the Apostle Paul highlight that triumph not only happens but surpasses our expectations because of God's Love. This verse fills us with hope and confidence as believers, reminding us that our trials allow God to demonstrate His power and affection.

Ultimately, knowing that we are conquerors in the battle brings strength and encouragement. It motivates us to continue fighting, aware that Christ has already secured victory. Every trial reminds us that God's Love is more significant, stronger, and more potent than any forces of Darkness. As believers, we are not victims but victorious individuals destined for greatness through God's transformative Love.

A narrative of being conquerors and standing empowered in battle is a powerful reminder of our strength and potential in our journey with God.

We can deepen our understanding of this truth by studying the teachings of known Bible scholars and Christian authors. In times of difficulty, we can take comfort in knowing that God's Love and strength will guide us through every challenge and empower us to emerge victorious. Let us hold tightly to God's promises and continue to walk in His Love, fully aware that we are conquerors and much more through Him.

Equip yourself with divine weapons. Faith, hope, Love, and truth.

We must arm ourselves with divine weapons in the struggle against the forces that try to lead us astray. Faith, hope, Love, and truth. These virtues are not ideas but powerful tools bestowed upon us by divine grace. They serve as unwavering strongholds as we face the battles within our minds and spirits, safeguarding us from the storms that threaten to overwhelm us.

Faith is the weapon in our arsenal; it represents unwavering trust in the Almighty. It embodies assurance of things hoped for and conviction of things Hebrews 11:1). Our unshakable faith in the promises of God and His flawless plan gives us the courage to move forward even when the path ahead is unclear. St. Augustine, a scholar of the Bible, once wrote, "Faith is believing in what we cannot see; its reward is seeing what we believe."" Through our faith, we find the strength to step out of our comfort zones and embrace the unknown, trusting that God is always by our side.

Hope, our weapon, empowers us to persevere in challenging times. It's not just thinking; it's confident anticipation that God will fulfil His promises. As the apostle Paul reminds us in Romans 15:13, ""May the God of hope fill you with all joy and peace as you trust in Him so that you may overflow with hope by the power of the Holy Spirit."" Hope allows us to look beyond our circumstances and grasp an eternal perspective. Charles Spurgeon beautifully described hope as a star that shines brightest during adversity.

Love, our weapon, surpasses them all. It is characterized by selflessness and sacrificial acts like Christ displayed on the cross for us.

This incredible Love not only comes from God and flows through us, but it also reaches out to touch the lives of others. The apostle Paul beautifully describes Love in his letter to the Corinthians: "Love is patient; Love is kind. It does not feel jealous. It does not brag; it is not arrogant"" (1 Corinthians 13:4). Through Love, we reflect the nature of God. Bring brightness into a world filled with Darkness. Martin Luther King Jr. Once stated, ""Darkness cannot overcome Darkness; only light can do that. Hate cannot conquer hate; only Love can.""

Moreover, truth acts as a shield that guards us against the deceptive tactics employed by our adversaries. In a world where falsehoods abound, seeking after truth enables us to discern God's will and distinguish between reality and fiction. The psalmist writes in Psalm 86:11, ""Teach me your ways, O Lord, so that I may rely on your faithfulness; give me a heart so that I may revere your name."" Truth liberates us. Grants us the wisdom needed to navigate life's intricate complexities.

The famous Christian author, C.S. Lewis, once expressed his fondness for tea and books, saying, ""I can never have a cup of tea that's too big or a book that's too long."" His words highlight the pursuit of truth and the constant thirst for knowledge.

When we arm ourselves with faith, hope, Love, and truth as tools, we can withstand the challenges that try to derail us. These virtues create a stronghold in the battles we face in our minds and spirits. Throughout history, known Bible scholars and Christian writers have emphasized the significance and power of these tools. By embracing them, we can find inspiration and encouragement while navigating life's obstacles with wisdom. Remember what the apostle Paul said, "And now these three remain faith, hope and Love. The greatest is love""

(1 Corinthians 13:13). May we incorporate these tools into our lives to empower ourselves and inspire others to walk with unwavering faith, enduring hope, selfless Love, and eternal truth.

Triumph doesn't come from human intelligence.

There is a struggle in spirituality, a battle between good and evil forces. Every believer is called to participate in this battle, fighting against the enemy schemes and staying strong in their faith. However, it's important to remember that victory in this fight doesn't come from human knowledge alone but from seeking divine guidance. The stories and experiences of those who have engaged in warfare serve as a reminder of God's unwavering faithfulness, transforming our challenges into blessings.

The Apostle Paul emphasizes this truth in his letter to the Corinthians, saying, "Our weapons for this battle are not physical but possess the power to demolish strongholds" (2 Corinthians 10:4 ESV). This verse reminds us that our fight isn't waged with tools or human wisdom but with the power that flows from God. The triumph we seek in warfare can only be attained by seeking divine counsel and following His guidance.

When confronted with battles, we must recognize the limits of our understanding and wisdom. Proverbs 14:12 states, "There may be ways that seem right, to us humans. They lead only to death" (ESV).

We may be tempted to rely on our understanding and develop strategies, but doing so can lead us astray. C.S. Lewis captures this limitation well in his book "Mere Christianity," stating, "God has infinite attention for each one of us. You are as alone with Him as if you were the only being He had ever created."

While human wisdom may falter, divine guidance remains steadfast. The book of Psalms reminds us, "He leads me in paths of righteousness for His name's sake" (Psalm 23;3 ESV). This verse beautifully encapsulates the essence of counsel to direct us towards righteousness and align us with God's will. The wisdom from counsel provides clarity, guidance, and strength when we face spiritual battles.

Throughout the Bible, we encounter inspiring stories of individuals who sought guidance and witnessed God's unwavering faithfulness in their struggles. David, a figure in biblical history, faced numerous challenges and spiritual battles throughout his life. As he affirms in Psalm 18:2, "The Lord is my rock and my fortress and my deliverer; my God, my rock in whom I take refuge; my shield and the horn of my salvation; my stronghold." David's triumph over Goliath, his triumph on the battlefield, and his rise to kingship exemplify God's faithfulness and strength in seeking divine guidance.

Ultimately, our struggles in warfare can be transformed into blessings through God's unwavering faithfulness. Romans 8:28 states, "We know that for those who love God, all things work together for good for those who are called according to his purpose" (ESV). Amidst our battles, we can confidently believe God is orchestrating everything for our ultimate good. The trials and challenges we face serve to refine and strengthen our faith while deepening our relationship with God.

Victory in warfare doesn't stem from human wisdom alone; instead, it comes from seeking divine counsel and placing unwavering trust in God's faithfulness.

By listening to the stories of characters and the accounts of faithful individuals, over time, we are reminded of how divine guidance can guide us towards triumph in our spiritual challenges. When we depend on God's wisdom and direction, our difficulties are turned into sources of blessings, demonstrating God's loyalty and drawing us nearer to Him.

Chapter Twelve
In His Kingdom Hope

Hope in God Promises

Finding Hope can be challenging in a world of uncertainty and fear. However, when we anchor our souls in the promises of God, we discover a steadfast and unwavering hope that empowers us to face life's challenges with courage and confidence. It explores the depth of God's promises, revealing the power that is unlocked when we build our lives upon His unchanging truth.

At the core of this chapter lies a belief that God's promises are not empty words but rather gateways to a life brimming with Hope, purpose, and significance. As Bruce K. Waltke, a Bible scholar, beautifully articulates, "The world may be full of broken human promises, but the promises of God are true and reliable." This profound truth is a guiding light of Hope, reminding us that amid life's ever-changing circumstances, there is an unwavering God who remains faithful to His promises.

Our Hope becomes shallow and uncertain when we perceive God as distant and indifferent. However, our Hope soars to heights once we grasp the depth of His love and faithfulness. Kingdom Hope aims to cultivate an intimate understanding of God's character by intertwining biblical truths. Together, let us paint a picture of our Heavenly Father.

A central theme explored in this chapter revolves around the concept of the kingdom of God. N.T. Wright, a theologian, beautifully articulates that the kingdom of God is not merely a phrase or coded language but a way to describe God's supreme authority breaking into our world. This eternal kingdom surpasses this world's systems and temporary nature, providing an unwavering foundation for our Hope. Kingdom Hope dives into how embracing this perspective can transform us and urges readers to align their lives with God's sovereign rule, thus unlocking the richness of Hope and purpose.

Moreover, this thought-provoking book delves into the significance of anchoring our souls in God's promises.

In his book "Anchoring Your Soul in the Storms of Life," Bill Crowder, an author and speaker, emphasizes that when our Hope is built upon God's promises, it remains steadfast even in the face of adversity. Within the pages of Kingdom Hope, readers are guided to develop an understanding of various promises mentioned in Scripture, such as God's promise of constant presence (Hebrews 13: 5) and the assurance of eternal life (1 John 2:25).

Drawing from years of study and personal experiences, I skilfully intertwine these promises into relatable narratives, showcasing their relevance and empowering nature even during life's darkest moments. Through stories highlighting triumph over challenges, accounts depicting God's faithfulness, and reflections on figures' lives, Kingdom Hope inspires readers to securely anchor their souls in God's promises, irrespective of their circumstances.

Anchoring Our Souls in God's Promises is a profoundly stirring exploration into Hope's transformative power grounded in God's unwavering assurances. I will take you on a journey to comprehend the depths of God's character, grasp the significance of His kingdom, and firmly anchor their souls in His truth.

By citing scholars of the Bible and acclaimed Christian writers, sharing some of my journey establishes a strong foundation of wisdom and profound insights. Together, let us embark on this journey, for in doing so, we will uncover an unwavering hope that is both inspiring and enriched with divine wisdom.

Harmonize them, transforming discord into a melody.

Amidst the symphony of life challenges, when despair seems to echo through its dissonant notes, it is essential to remember that God's promises to possess the power to harmonize and metamorphose this chaos into a captivating melody. The unwavering sovereign offers hope from His kingdom to all who find solace in Him. Drawing upon biblical scholars and revered Christian authors, this paragraph will explore the inspirational message infused with Godly wisdom that celebrates the transformative capability of God's promises. It will guide us from despair towards Hope.

Life often presents us with trials, difficulties, and moments of despair. In the face of adversity, our human hearts may be enticed by despondency. However, during these moments, we are reminded of our need to seek refuge in the assurances provided by God.

Renowned Christian writer Charles H. Spurgeon once penned these words; "When troubles arise, God becomes a fortress for the oppressed" (Spurgeon, 1865, p. 236). This profound statement reminds us that even in our moments of despair, God is always there to provide solace and renewed Hope.

The promises of God can be likened to melodies that bring tranquillity and unity to our hearts. The esteemed theologian J.I. Packer beautifully captured this effect by stating, "The promises delivered by the Spirit of God bring inner assurance and a soothing sense of calmness, turning the chaotic symphony within us into a melodious masterpiece" (Packer, 1973, p. 102). This imagery serves as a testament that when we anchor ourselves in the promises of God, they create an uplifting melody that comforts our troubled souls.

In the darkest depths of despair, holding onto the unwavering and everlasting Hope offered by God's kingdom is crucial. As the apostle Paul assures us, "Faith is being sure of what we hope for and certain of what we do not see" (Hebrews

11:1 English Standard Version). This biblical truth reminds us that when despair threatens to overwhelm us entirely, our faith in God's promises sustains our Hope.

To cultivate optimism and find solace amidst the chaos of despair, seeking guidance and wisdom from Christian sources is essential. A.W. Tozer, a theologian, emphasized the significance of aligning our hearts with God's truth. He says, "Through instruction, we can experience the transformative power of God's promises that bring harmony instead of discord into our lives" (Tozer, 1948, p. 79).

A beacon of Hope and renewal.

When life symphony echoes, with notes of hopelessness, God's promises become a beacon of Hope and renewal. Our souls discover shelter and tranquillity by anchoring ourselves in Him—the unwavering King. We uncover the harmonizing influence that God's promises possess within our lives. Let us grasp the Hope God offers and allow His promises to metamorphose despair into a harmonious composition filled with peace and certainty.

Place your trust in the promises of the Almighty King, discover Hope in the darkest moments, and let your innermost be enlightened. This is what encompasses Kingdom Hope. In a world filled with uncertainties, doubts, and challenges, we must firmly anchor ourselves in the assurances given by our ruler, God Himself. Then, can we uncover a hope that transcends all despair and banishes the shadows that threaten to consume our spirits? Kingdom Hope carries a truth explored by esteemed biblical scholars and Christian writers, offering us invaluable wisdom to navigate our spiritual journey.

One of the principles of Kingdom Hope can be found in the book of Hebrews. The writer encourages us to stay firm in our faith and have unwavering confidence in God's promises; "We have this hope as an anchor, for the soul, firm and secure. It enters the sanctuary behind the curtain" (Hebrews 6:19-20 NIV). Here, an anchor is used as a metaphor, symbolizing the steadfastness of our Hope in Christ.

The anchor serves as both a source of stability during life's storms and a connection to the presence of God. When we focus on Jesus, who goes before us, we can embark on a journey knowing He has already prepared the way.

Echoing this sentiment, A.W. Tozer, a theologian, expresses that Hope is the refuge for our soul's fears. It surpasses circumstances and appearances to discover the faithfulness of God (Tozer, A.W. The Root of the Righteous). Tozer emphasizes that Hope is not bound by changing tides but instead finds its foundation in God's faithfulness. Therefore, Kingdom Hope encourages us to shift our perspective from temporary to eternal and transient to enduring.

Moreover, Kingdom Hope urges us to delve into the depths of our hearts. It prompts introspection that goes beyond surface-level examination and reaches into the core of our being.

In Psalm 139, the writer offers a prayer saying, "Dear God please search my heart and understand my thoughts. Help me recognize any behaviours within me and guide me towards a path of eternal goodness" (Psalm 139:23-24 NASB). This heartfelt plea demonstrates the psalmist's awareness of the importance of self-reflection. Allowing God to reveal hidden anxieties or sinful tendencies. By engaging in this process, we can nurture Kingdom Hope by acknowledging our vulnerabilities and surrendering them to God's transformative power.

Rick Warren delves into the significance of this journey in his book "The Purpose Driven Life." He emphasizes the need to regularly ask ourselves questions like, "What exerts control over my life? Where do I place my hope? What am I truly relying on?" (Warren, Rick. The Purpose Driven Life). By posing these queries, we confront the idols and distractions that often undermine our Hope. Through self-evaluation, we can realign our hearts with God's purpose and discover a renewed sense of Hope deeply rooted in Him.

Ultimately, Kingdom Hope serves as a catalyst for transformation that propels us towards lives filled with meaning and fulfilment.

In times of hardship and despair, we genuinely understand the power of Hope. Throughout history, figures like Moses and David have shown us the strength of faith serving as guiding lights towards divine grace.

When faced with adversity, these biblical icons have consistently demonstrated a belief in God's promises, inspiring believers throughout different eras. Their grasp of the promises made by God acted as a guiding force leading humanity towards the shores of grace. In this paragraph, we will explore the wisdom these biblical figures convey and how their unwavering faith can encourage those facing their challenges. By referencing Bible scholars and Christian authors, we will delve into the inspiring nature of their stories and reflect on the relevance of their messages in our lives today.

Our trials are not battles but opportunities for God's grace to shine.

In times of hardship, Moses emerged as a figure who embodied Hope in the face of overwhelming circumstances. Moses clung to divine promises from birth to his leadership in leading the Israelites to the Promised Land. As noted, Bible scholar R.T. France explains, "Moses found the strength to persevere by keeping his focus on a God who served as his ultimate source of encouragement." Through the narrative of Exodus, Moses demonstrated unwavering trust in God, enabling him to overcome insurmountable obstacles. His faith inspired the Israelites, reminding them about the power of Hope and God's faithfulness.

Similarly, David—a psalmist who transitioned from being a shepherd boy to becoming a king—encountered numerous trials throughout his life. During these moments, David poured his heart solely into God and found solace in Him alone.

Christian writer Beth Moore mentioned that David's belief in God was a steadfast foundation during turbulent times. The Psalms he composed showcase his trust in the Lord even amidst moments of despair. David's profound comprehension of God's promises and his unwavering commitment to His faithfulness offered solace and strength to generations.

The faith demonstrated by Moses and David echoes with meaning in our present lives. Their experiences provide lessons on navigating difficult periods while relying on God's assurances. Biblical scholar Walter Brueggemann confirms that "the stories of Moses and David confront us with the understanding that hope remains a force even in moments of despair shaping our perspective." Their narratives remind us that Hope is not merely a fleeting emotion but an anchoring force that keeps us firmly rooted in God's promises.

As believers, we must internalize the wisdom imparted by these figures. When we lack Hope, despair can occur. Paralyze us. Conversely, embracing faith dispels darkness. Infuses our lives with renewed purpose and determination. Turning to the life stories of Moses and David reminds us that our trials are not battles but opportunities for God's grace to shine through.

Their unwavering trust teaches us to perceive our challenges as stones towards a more fantastic future, allowing resilience to shape our character and deepen our connection with God.

Amid times of despair, biblical figures like Moses and David inspire us. Their unwavering trust and hope to remind them of God's promises and faithfulness. By following their example, we can navigate through trials, believing God's grace will guide us to triumph. Let us embrace the wisdom these biblical icons share, knowing that faith remains unshakeable even in the darkest storms, like an anchor lighting up our path towards lasting victory.

Nurture our faith by grounding ourselves in the soil of His eternal truth.

We actively seek out His promises to foster anticipation in God's kingdom. Like attentive gardeners caring for their crops, we must nurture our faith by grounding ourselves in the soil of His timeless truth. This profound insight highlights our power and responsibility as believers to cultivate and nurture our relationship with God. In doing so, we discover a hope that transcends all understanding.

In the book of Jeremiah, there is a passage where the prophet talks about a time when God's people would come back from exile and rebuild what was destroyed. The Lord declares, "For I am aware of the plans I have for you plans to bring prosperity and not harm, plans to give you hope and a future" (Jeremiah 29:11). This promise of Hope clearly shows that God is a deity of restoration and redemption. We are not simply expected to wait for this Hope to manifest but actively pursue it just like a gardener takes care of their crops.

Eugene Peterson discusses Hope in his book "A Long Obedience in the Direction ", stating that it is not merely an added decoration for aesthetic purposes in biblical faith. Instead, Hope serves as an adrenaline shot, a blood transfusion, rather than acting as a sedative. Peterson highlights the importance of viewing Hope as a pursuit rather than having a passive mindset. We must plant seeds of faith and nourish our relationship with God while trusting in His promises and living obediently.

The Apostle Paul, in his letter addressed to the Colossians, advises them to continue following Christ just as they initially accepted Him as their Lord. In the Bible verse Colossians 2:6-7, the apostle Paul uses the metaphor of roots sinking into fertile soil to illustrate the importance of being firmly grounded in Christ. By establishing this connection, our faith can flourish and face challenges with confidence and gratitude.

Author Lili Smith emphasizes in her book "Living Hope: Steps to Nurture Kingdom Hope" that nurturing Hope requires discipline, commitment, and surrender. It involves seeking God's presence, aligning our hearts with His will, and trusting His faithfulness. Smith underscores the need for efforts on our part to cultivate a receptive heart that embraces God's truth.

These texts and writings urge us to act rather than passively observe our faith. We are called to engage in the incredible journey of pursuing God's promises and experiencing His Hope.

As we sow and nurture the seeds of faith through prayer, studying Scripture, and engaging in fellowship, we witness the transformation that occurs through God's love. Our souls become like gardens, serving as a testament to His faithfulness and an inspiration for those around us.

Nurturing Hope in God's kingdom requires effort. We have been entrusted with tending to our faith as diligent gardeners tend to their crops. By rooting ourselves in the soil of God's eternal truth, we can discover a hope that surpasses all understanding and cultivate a steadfast faith that cannot be shaken. Through the wisdom found in texts writings by inspired authors and the examples set by faithful believers, we are encouraged to pursue God's promises actively and consistently. As we do so, we are transformed into vessels of Hope. Serve as sources of inspiration for others seeking nourishment from the abundant love of God.

Lighthouse guiding us safely through storms.

Hope shines bright amidst despair like a lighthouse guiding us safely through storms. Anchor your soul in God's promises; He is our beacon, illuminating the path towards His everlasting Kingdom. Keep your soul anchored in God's promises as He guides us towards His eternal Kingdom. In moments of struggle and despair, it can be easy to lose sight of any glimmer of Hope. Life storms may seem overwhelming, leaving us feeling lost and disheartened. However, during these moments, Hope shines brightest, reminding us of the everlasting promises made by our loving Creator.

The concept of Hope runs within the pages of the Holy Bible. From the Old to the New Testament, we come across stories of individuals who clung to hope amidst immense despair. Consider the story of Job as an example. Despite enduring suffering and losing everything dear to him, Job remained steadfast in his faith towards God. In Job 13:15, he declares, "Even if He kills me, I will still trust in Him." Jobs' unwavering Hope in God's faithfulness reminds us that even when going through our darkest trials, we can find Hope in the promises made by our Heavenly Father.

Known biblical scholar and Christian author J.I. Packer once said, "Hope is a vital and fundamental element in the Christian life. "Packer's words reflect that Hope is not merely a passing feeling but an essential element of our faith. This Hope is not based on thinking or empty positivity but on the solid foundation of God's unwavering faithfulness. The Apostle Paul confirms this truth in Romans 15:13, saying, "May the God of hope fill you with all joy and peace as you trust in him so that you may abound in hope by the power of the Holy Spirit."

The power of Hope lies in its ability to anchor our souls to God's promises. Charles H. Spurgeon wrote, "A solid character is not easily shaken once established. It is like a house built on a rock." When we place our Hope in God and His promises, we establish a foundation to withstand life's storms. As a lighthouse guides and protects ships during storms, God promises to shine as a beacon of Hope, showing us the path towards eternal security and peace.

The book of Psalms contains verses that express the Hope we can find in God. Psalm 43:5 asks, "Why are you downcast, O my soul? Why so disturbed within me? "Place your trust in God, for I will continue to express my gratitude towards Him as He's my rescuer and the one I rely on." This psalmist inspires us to find solace in God's assurances, diverting our attention from the gloom that envelops us and redirecting it towards the optimism that arises from having faith in Him.

Indeed, the Bible presents instances of Hope shining through moments of despair. Whether it's the faith exhibited by Abraham, who believed in God's pledge to bless him with a child even during his advanced years or the resurrection of Jesus Christ that brought Hope to a world engulfed in sin, God has consistently proven trustworthy to those who place their Hope in Him. As we contemplate these tales and ponder the wisdom shared by scholars and writers, we discover the strength to embrace Hope even during our darkest hours.

When we ground our spirits in God's assurances, we discover a beacon of Hope that lights the path towards His eternal Kingdom. As we navigate life's storms, remember Hebrews 6 19, which states, "We have this hope as an anchor, for the soul, firm and secure." May we constantly draw strength from our Heavenly Father's promises. May His enduring Hope carry us through every trial and tribulation, guiding us towards a future brimming with everlasting joy and peace.

CHAPTER THIRTEEN
IN HIS KINGDOM EXPANSION

SHARING AND MULTIPLICATION

The idea of expanding His Kingdom has always been central to God's plan for humanity's redemption. Right from the start, God desired to establish His Kingdom on Earth and appointed humans as stewards to fulfil this purpose. This narrative delves into the vision of sharing and multiplying God's Kingdom, inspiring Christians to actively participate in advancing His reign on earth. Drawing upon wisdom insights from renowned scholars and authors, we explore how expanding the Kingdom brings hope, restoration, and fulfilment of divine purposes.

The foundation of expanding the Kingdom lies in Jesus Christ Himself and His Great Commission. In Matthew 28:19-20, Jesus commands His disciples, saying, "Therefore go and make disciples of all nations baptising them in the name of the Father and of the Son and of the Holy Spirit teaching them to obey everything I have commanded you." These words are not suggestions but a divine mandate emphasising the urgency and importance of sharing news about God's Kingdom.

To truly understand what it means to expand the Kingdom, we must grasp its essence—the reality of God's rule. The concept of the Kingdom of God goes beyond a location or territory; it is about the reign and authority of God manifesting in the lives of those who have been redeemed. Theologian N.T. Wright supports this perspective by stating that the Kingdom involves rescuing lost souls and transforming the world through saved individuals acting as change agents.

Expanding the Kingdom is not accomplished solely through human effort but by faithfully relying on God. In his book "Experiencing God ", Henry Blackaby reminds us that Kingdom expansion happens when we actively participate in God's work. By surrendering ourselves to Him, we become instruments for His purpose, allowing Him to work through us. As we abide in Him, we cultivate the fruits of the Spirit in our lives, which naturally draw others into His Kingdom.

Looking at the church as an inspiring example, we see how they embraced their calling to share and multiply the Kingdom of God. In the book of Acts, we witness how boldly proclaiming the Gospel and being led by the Holy Spirit resulted in expansion. The Apostle Paul captures the essence of Kingdom expansion in his letter to the Philippians, declaring, "I can do all things through Him who strengthens me" (Philippians 4:13). Paul's unwavering faith empowered him to overcome challenges, fearlessly spread the Gospel and establish churches across the Mediterranean region.

Moreover, the vision of expanding God's Kingdom is intricately connected to bringing about His reign on earth. In his book "Evangelism and the Sovereignty of God," author J.I. Packer highlights that expanding the Kingdom involves sharing the Gospel and actively addressing issues. While proclaiming the Good News remains paramount, it is equally important to combat societal injustices. Alleviate human suffering, ultimately reflecting the love, justice and mercy values that define God's Kingdom.

Embracing the concept of advancing God's Kingdom through sharing and multiplying it is a calling that draws us deeper into His purposes. By following the Great Commission, understanding the nature of His Kingdom, and relying on His wisdom and strength, we become agents of transformative change in individuals and society. Inspired by the church example and our divine mandate, we engage in evangelism, social activism, and discipleship—bringing forth God's Kingdom on earth as it is in heaven.

The actual expansion of God's Kingdom begins within our hearts.

In essence, the actual expansion of God's Kingdom begins within our hearts. When we share love with others, we effectively share Him with them. May our actions always convey His message so His Kingdom multiplies across all corners of our world.

The actual expansion of the Kingdom commences from within our hearts. It is not determined by the size of our following or the grandeur of our structures. Instead, by the depth of love we have for one another. When we share passion, we are sharing God. Love stands as the commandment embodying the essence of our faith and serving as the wellspring for genuine unity among us. Echoing Jesus' words in John 13:34-35, He declared, "I give you a commandment: Love one another. As I have loved you, you are also to love one another. By this, all people will know that you are my disciples if you love one another."

To truly love as Jesus did is a life-altering experience. It necessitates a willingness to release our desires and embrace the needs of others wholeheartedly. This entails seeking justice for those who face oppression, comforting those with hearts and offering forgiveness to those who have wronged us. As we embody Christ's love in action, our deeds become a testimony that conveys His message of hope, redemption, and salvation.

In his book titled "The Power of Love," Bishop Michael Curry emphasises the profound significance of love as the cornerstone of our faith. He refers to the teachings of Jesus and the Christian communities to remind us that passion encompasses emotions and actions. This extraordinary force can bring healing, reconciliation, and lasting transformation. Bishop Curry expresses, "When we love as God loves, we become a vessel of His grace, a conduit through which His Kingdom spreads and multiplies."

N.T. Wright believes that the expansion of God's Kingdom throughout the world is not an abstract theological concept but a tangible reality visible through the deeds of believers. Wright argues that God's Kingdom is not confined to a place or time but is an active and transformative power working towards reconciliation, restoration, and redemption. He writes, "The Kingdom of God represents God's supreme authority breaking into our age through Jesus Christ's life, death and resurrection. It is here, with us now—breaking barriers, bringing light into darkness—and fulfilling God's earthly purposes."

Once we grasp the essence of this Kingdom, we realise that it is not an exclusive club reserved for a select few but an inclusive community where all who desire to follow Christ are welcomed with open arms.

The expansion of the Kingdom knows no bounds, encompassing people and nations worldwide. As noted by author and theologian Henri Nouwen in his book "In the Name of Jesus, "We are called to extend our focus beyond our needs and desires, embracing the needs of others. Nouwen points out how society often promotes individualism, competition, and success. In contrast, the Kingdom of God encourages community, cooperation, and selfless service. This shift requires humility, vulnerability, and a willingness to let go of agendas.

Actual expansion of the Kingdom begins within each person's heart. When we share love with others, we are sharing God's love. Our actions driven by Christ's love become a testimony that conveys His message of redemption, hope and salvation. As we embrace others' needs and strive to extend Christ's love, His Kingdom multiplies worldwide. Let us heed the words of Apostle Paul in Galatians 5:22-23; "But the fruit of the Spirit is love, joy peace patience kindness goodness faithfulness gentleness, self-control; against things, there is no law."

May our actions always reflect His message.

The Kingdom Mandate urges us to move, not merely walk and to speak boldly rather than whisper. Let us share His teachings because, through Personal Evangelism, each soul we touch brings blessings. This powerful concept is deeply rooted in the wisdom of the Scriptures. It continues to resonate today, motivating believers to step out of their comfort zones and proclaim God's love and redemption. As the Apostle Paul declared in Romans 10:14, "How can they call on Him if they have not believed? How can they believe in Him if they have never heard? How will they hear without someone preaching?"

The Kingdom Mandate serves as a call to action—a divine commission given to believers to spread the Gospel throughout all nations. In this mandate lies the responsibility to follow in Jesus' footsteps and a sense of urgency and passion as we run this race. Throughout the pages of the Bible, we come across examples of men and women who embraced this calling and made history.

One figure from the Bible is Elijah, a prophet. In 1 Kings 18, we read an inspiring story of Elijah's encounter with the prophets of Baal on Mount Carmel. Elijah's passion and fearlessness in challenging the prophets and calling upon heavenly fire to consume his offering left an unforgettable impression on all who witnessed it. This account serves as a reminder that our God is a consuming fire, and when we step out in faith, He will display His power, drawing people closer to Him.

The significance of evangelism is further emphasised in Jesus' teachings. In Matthew 28:19-20, known as the Great Commission, Jesus commands His disciples to "Go and make disciples of all nations baptising them in the name of the Father and of the Son and of the Holy Spirit teaching them to observe all that I have commanded you." Jesus instructs His followers to spread His message and guide individuals towards an understanding of their faith journey.

Delving into evangelism would only be complete with discussing Apostle Paul's impact. His tireless missionary travels, captivating sermons and unwavering dedication to spreading the Gospel serve as an example to believers across generations. The words of Paul in 1 Corinthians 9:16 reflect the essence of evangelism: "For if I preach the Gospel, I have no reason to boast for necessity is laid upon me. Woe to me if I do not preach the Gospel!"

Christian authors and biblical scholars have extensively discussed the importance of evangelism in disseminating God's Word and fulfilling the mandate of His Kingdom. In his book Ashamed of the Gospel, Dr. John MacArthur writes, "Personal evangelism is a command, for all believers and an integral part of carrying out His Kingdoms mission." MacArthur highlights its urgency and responsibility and emphasises that believers are entrusted with proclaiming Christ to a lost world.

Similarly, an evangelist, Billy Graham, said, "The Gospel brings good news only when it reaches people in time." Graham fully grasped the nature of personal evangelism and comprehended the eternal consequences of sharing the message of salvation. Throughout his ministry, he tirelessly preached about salvation. He urged individuals to respond willingly to God's calling.

The impact of evangelism extends far beyond individual conversions. As each soul touched by the power of the Gospel undergoes change, a ripple effect ensues.

Lives are transformed, families find healing, communities experience changes, and the blessings of God multiply abundantly. Every person who embraces Christ represents His love, bearing fruit and spreading His Kingdom.

The Kingdom Mandate urges believers to go beyond walking or speaking softly; it encourages them to run and shout with conviction. Evangelism is vital to fulfilling this mandate because every soul touched creates exponential blessings. Drawing inspiration from figures like Elijah and the teachings of Jesus and the Apostle Paul, we are called to step forward with faith and confidently proclaim the Gospel. The insights shared by Bible scholars and Christian authors further emphasise the significance and urgency of personal evangelism. Let us wholeheartedly embrace this mission and share the incredible message of God's love and redemption. By doing we actively participate in advancing the eternal work of His Kingdom. May our endeavours bring glory to God's name while leading souls into His everlasting embrace.

The One who has the power to move mountains stands by our side.

In our pursuit of expanding the Kingdom, we may come across challenges. These challenges can manifest as mountains symbolising obstacles, opposition or even our fears and doubts. However, it's crucial to remember that the One who has the power to move mountains stands by our side. His love is a guiding light that empowers us to overcome these challenges and fulfil our divine purpose.

As we delve deeper into this subject, we should seek wisdom and insights from respected Bible scholars and Christian authors. One such scholar is Dr. Warren W. Wiersbe, who reminds us in his book "Be Strong; Putting God's Power to Work in Your Life" that God doesn't expect us to face mountains alone. He promises to be with us every step of the way. These words from Wiersbe reflect that when we trust in God's presence, we tap into a strength that enables us to conquer any obstacle. The psalmist also affirms this in Psalm 18:32 when he says, "It is God who equips me with strength and keeps my path secure."

Drawing inspiration from authors, Charles Stanley emphasises in his book, "The Power of God Love," that God's love guides us and provides incredible strength. According to Stanley, God's love can overcome any obstacle in our path. It empowers us to face adversity with unwavering courage and faith. The love of God goes beyond comprehension and can conquer any challenge we encounter.

When we encounter mountains in life, we must recognise that these challenges are not occurrences but opportunities for personal growth and transformation. In his book "The Purpose Driven Life", Rick Warren explores the purpose behind these mountains. Warren suggests that God never wastes a hurt or a mountain;

instead, He utilises them to shape us, teach us lessons, and prepare us for His divine plan. This perspective encourages us to shift our mindset from perceiving mountains as obstacles to embracing them as stones on our journey towards fulfilling our destiny.

In the Gospel of Matthew 17:20, Jesus tells His disciples about the power of faith. He states that even if one possesses faith small, as a mustard seed, they can command a mountain to move from one place to another with just their words.

This verse serves as a reminder that nothing will be impossible for us. It emphasises that the key to overcoming challenges lies in placing our trust in God's love and power rather than the size of our faith. By relying on His strength, we can triumph over any obstacles that come our way, like Jesus Christ exemplified unwavering faith and trust throughout His ministry. He faced physical, emotional, and spiritual mountains but never doubted God's presence with Him. In John 16:33, Jesus encourages us to have confidence by assuring us that although we will encounter troubles in this world, He has already overcome them.

As we strive for Kingdom Expansion, we must acknowledge that mountains may arise. However, we must remember that God, who can move mountains figuratively and literally, stands beside us. He is always ready to empower us with His love and provide guidance. Trusting in Jesus' words and maintaining unwavering faith, like Him, we can conquer any challenge or obstacle that comes our way.

Let us gather our courage and allow the guiding light of His love to lead and empower us on this journey of spreading His Kingdom.

Expanding the Kingdom goes beyond numbers; it touches hearts.

In the tapestry of life, we often become fixated on numbers. We measure success by achievements, bank account balances, or social media followers. However, when expanding God's Kingdom, we must rise above evaluations and adopt a divine perspective. As the wise saying goes, expanding the Kingdom goes beyond numbers; it touches hearts. This profound truth reminds us to focus not on outcomes but on our actions' profound impact on others' lives.

It is crucial to understand that expanding God's Kingdom is not simply an endeavour. It is not about gaining followers or converting the masses. Instead, it is a journey where every interaction holds great significance. Love, which serves as God's currency, is the key that opens others' hearts. Through love and kindness, we can inspire and touch those around us.

Many scholars who study the Bible and authors who write about Christianity have explored this timeless wisdom. The Apostle Paul, in his letter to the Corinthians, expresses this idea when he says, "Even if I give away everything I own and sacrifice my body but don't have love, it means nothing" (1 Corinthians 13:3 NIV). Paul highlights that even the most significant sacrifices hold no significance without love. Love sets us apart. It enables us to make a lasting impact on those around us.

John Paul II, an influential Christian figure in modern times, also echoes this sentiment in his book "Crossing the Threshold of Hope." He states, "Christianity is not merely a collection of truths to believe in or rules to follow; above all else, it is a love story." John Paul II reminds us that Christianity is not about rigid doctrines but rather an incredible journey of love. Through this story of love, we can touch people's hearts. Bring them closer to God.

The words of renowned Christian author C.S. Lewis also provide wisdom. In his book "Mere Christianity ", Lewis ponders the idea that as we allow God to take control of our lives, we discover ourselves because He is the one who created us. He envisioned every individual that you and I were meant to be. Lewis beautifully captures the essence of expanding God's Kingdom. It involves experiencing the depth of God's love and allowing it to shape us into our authentic versions. As we embrace this truth, our lives become a testament to the divine love that transcends the limitations of this existence.

It's essential to remember that the impact of our actions, driven by love, holds significance. Jesus emphasised the importance of storing treasures in heaven, protecting them from decay or theft (Matthew 6:20 ESV). When we invest in expanding God's Kingdom through acts of love, these treasures remain untouched by time or worldly challenges. Their value surpasses any material wealth or achievements.

Let us embark on a journey towards expanding God's Kingdom that goes beyond numbers. Let us strive to touch the hearts of those around us with love because it's the currency of God.

By investing in acts of love, we can reap everlasting rewards beyond any measurements of success in this earthly realm. Expanding God's Kingdom is a beautiful love story that allows us to embrace our true selves. Focusing solely on worldly achievements lets us direct our attention towards the profound impact we can have on the lives of others as we strive to bring them closer to God and experience His boundless love.

A prayer is not a whisper; it resounds like a mighty lion.

Through Prayer, we ignite the growth and spread of God's Kingdom because He responds when His people passionately seek His presence. A prayer holds power—it is not merely a whisper. Still, it resonates like the mighty roar of a lion within the spiritual realm. It serves as a tool for igniting the expansion of God's Kingdom and bringing about extraordinary transformations. When we engage in unwavering Prayer, fervently seeking God's presence, we open doors for intervention and align ourselves with His will on earth as it is in heaven. This concept finds its roots deeply embedded in God's Word and echoes throughout the teachings of Bible scholars and Christian writers. It serves as a reminder of the incredible potential inherent in heartfelt Prayer.

In Matthew's book, chapter 7:8, Jesus guides His followers: "If you ask for something, it will be given to you; if you seek, you will find it; if you knock, the door will open. Those who ask to receive what they seek; those who search find what they need; Those who knock on the door find it open." This profound promise captures the essence of Prayer. It reminds us that we have access to God's presence, and when we earnestly seek Him, He will respond to our prayers. As a known biblical scholar, J.C. Ryle affirms, "Prayer is mankind's most powerful weapon. It is a key that unlocks God's promises and unleashes His power in our lives."

Apostle Paul encourages believers in Philippians 4:6-7 by saying, "Don't worry about anything; instead, pray about everything. Tell God what you need and thank Him for all He has done. Then, you will experience God's peace, which surpasses understanding. It will guard your hearts and minds as you live in Christ Jesus." This passage highlights the impact of Prayer. It serves as a way for us to present our requests before God while also providing a source of peace and assurance.

As Christian author Andrew Murray emphasised, Prayer is not about making requests; it involves embracing God's will instead of our own. It's about aligning our hearts with God's heart.

When we adopt a posture of Prayer, we align ourselves with God's purposes and become vessels for expanding His Kingdom. E.M. Bounds, a known Christian author, once remarked that the Wesleyan movement transformed the world through continuous, persistent, and unwavering Prayer. This statement highlights the power of passionate Prayer in bringing about radical change. The fervent prayers of John and Charles Wesley and their fellow believers led to a revival that impacted lives and ignited a movement spanning generations.

What makes Prayer so profound is not the words we speak but also the deep connection we establish with our Heavenly Father. Through Prayer, we cultivate a relationship that allows us to experience the depth of His love and power. As eloquently expressed by C.S. Lewis, Prayer (asking for things) forms only a tiny part of it; confession and penitence serve as its threshold, adoration as its sanctuary while being, in the presence of God, becomes nourishment for our souls.

The idea that Prayer is not merely a whisper but a powerful force in the realm inspires and encourages believers to engage in unwavering Prayer. This understanding, grounded in Scripture and supported by respected Bible scholars and Christian authors, reaffirms Prayer's inherent power and potential. When we wholeheartedly seek God's presence, we open doors for His intervention and contribute to expanding His Kingdom. By embracing the impact of Prayer and aligning our hearts with God's will, we become vessels through which His purposes are fulfilled on earth. Let us, therefore, persistently seek His presence through Prayer and witness the works of our mighty God.

His Kingdom is not a one-time choice but a life choice commitment.

Embarking on a journey into God's life-changing Kingdom is an experience that encompasses every aspect of our existence. It is a journey characterised by faith, hope and love—guided by the wisdom in God's Word and inspired by the Holy Spirit. As we surrender ourselves to God's sovereignty, we find solace in knowing that we are valued members of His Kingdom, where He reigns with boundless love and mercy.

Throughout this journey, we discover our identities as children of God who have been redeemed and cherished by His grace.

In his writings, N.T. Wright beautifully captures the essence of living as a people embodying God's Kingdom. This understanding completely transforms our perspective. It fuels our passion to seek and embrace God's Kingdom in every aspect of our existence. Undoubtedly, as we navigate through the realm of God's Kingdom, we inevitably encounter challenges and trials. Nonetheless, we can find solace in the words of the esteemed author C.S. Lewis, who reminds us that hardships are not meant to punish us but draw us closer to God Himself. In these moments, we learn to rely on His strength and wisdom, knowing He accompanies us every step.

As we continue this journey, we must strive for a relationship with God that can only be attained through fervent Prayer and dedicated study of His Word. The Apostle Paul emphasises this significance in his letter to the Ephesians by urging us to grow in all aspects to become more like Christ, who leads us forward. This growth benefits both ourselves. Contributes to the advancement of God's Kingdom here, on earth.

Furthermore, as we traverse the realm of God's Kingdom, we must share His message of love and redemption with those who have yet to experience His transformative power. As the Apostle Peter reminds us, we are called to be a particular community, a revered group and a sacred nation. By living lives that embody God's goodness and extending His love to others, we become vessels through which His Kingdom can touch the lives of those around us.

Ultimately, our journey through God's Kingdom leads us to comprehend His purpose for our existence. As Rick Warren, an author, eloquently puts it, we are creations of God's Kingdom, intricately designed for specific purposes and equipped with unique talents. When we embrace this truth. Align our lives with God's divine plan, an overwhelming sense of fulfilment and joy engulfs us—a feeling that surpasses all human understanding.

Embarking on this life-altering expedition through God's Kingdom invites us to live out our faith passionately, courageously, and selflessly. It presents us with an opportunity to transform God's love and grace while becoming agents of His Kingdom here on earth. Let us take heed of the words spoken by Maximilian Kolbe—a renowned Christian author—who once stated that indifference is the most lethal poison in our time.

"Shall we embark on this adventure with hearts and unwavering dedication, persistently seeking to establish God's Kingdom? Let us wholeheartedly embrace the obstacles, recognising that it is in our vulnerabilities where God's strength truly shines. May we extend His love and redeeming message to a world yearning for hope."

In the realm of His Kingdom, we discover meaning, happiness, and everlasting existence. While we travel through the realm of God, may we find inspiration in the wisdom within His Word and the stories shared by those who came before us? Let us navigate our path with faith, hope and love while keeping our gaze fixed upon the glory that awaits us in God's loving embrace.

As we near the end of this journey within God's altering Kingdom, may you feel empowered, inspired, and equipped to prioritise seeking His Kingdom above all else in every aspect of your life. Remember that seeking His Kingdom is not a one-time choice but a life choice commitment in nurturing your relationship with Him and aligning yourself with His divine purpose. May you encounter joy, meaning and satisfaction as you fully embrace His sovereign rule. Now venture forth. Radiate His light as you embark upon this extraordinary expedition!

Epilogue

As I sit down to write every chapter, "In His Kingdom ", I can't help but feel overwhelmed by the incredible journey I've been on since the day I embraced, believed in and embraced living in His kingdom. The pages of this book have beautifully captured my transformation, the challenges I've faced, and the triumphs I've experienced. Now, as we reach this concluding part, let me share with you my profound journey with God's kingdom and how it has profoundly impacted my life.

The kingdom of God is like an ocean that stretches infinitely before us, brimming with immeasurable treasures. It is a realm defined by love, endless grace, and unfathomable wisdom. In the stages of my journey, I found myself standing at its shores—hesitant to plunge into the depths of this majestic domain. Doubts and fears held me back. Within me resonated God's gentle voice, compelling me to take that leap of faith.

With trembling steps but unwavering trust in Him, I finally submerged myself in His kingdom. Oh, what wonders awaited beneath those waters! The very ground upon which I tread was transformed into a path guiding me towards an unforeseen destiny.

I came to realize that God's kingdom is not an abstract idea but a vibrant reality that beckons to be explored.

Every step of my journey was filled with lessons, trials, and unexpected blessings. The path could have been smoother. Some tempests threatened to throw me off course, moments of doubt that crept into my mind, and temptations that enticed me away from the path. In those challenging moments, I drew strength from the unwavering knowledge that God's kingdom stands firm and unshakeable.

The deeper I immersed myself in God's kingdom, the more I witnessed His hand at work in my life. He revealed Himself through the warmth of a sunrise on a morning, through the gentle whispers of the wind that brought solace to my troubled heart, and through the embrace of loved ones who supported me during every trial. Each moment served as a testament to His faithfulness, love, and boundless power as King.

Embarking on this journey with God's kingdom taught me the beauty of surrender. As I relinquished my desires, ambitions, and plans to Him, I discovered His perfect purpose unfolding in my life. There were instances when His plans appeared contrary to mine; however, I learned to trust in His wisdom and timing. The challenges and obstacles I encountered along the way helped shape my character, strengthen my beliefs, and deepen my dependence on Him.

Within God's realm, I discovered a purpose that went beyond my self-interest. He called me to be a vessel of His love and kindness, reaching out to those who are tired and oppressed, offering hope to the hopeless, and extending forgiveness to the broken. As I embraced this calling, I witnessed incredible miracles unfold before my eyes. Lives were transformed, hearts were healed, and souls were liberated. The power of His realm became evident in every action I took.

Today, as I look back on my journey, with gratitude and wonderment. God's realm is not confined by time or space; it extends beyond the pages of this book. It is a reality that each one of us can experience if we choose to embark on this journey. So, reader, let this conclusion be an invitation for you to join me in exploring the depths of His realm.

May you find the courage to take that leap of faith and trust in the One who holds the universe in His hands.

May you uncover the hidden treasures that lie beneath the surface, and may you feel inspired to share the love, joy and peace that only God's kingdom can offer. Although challenges may arise along your journey, remember that God is by your side at every step, guiding, protecting, and empowering you to lead a life that brings honour to His name.

So, my exploration of God's kingdom continues. The path ahead may be uncertain. It is filled with hope. I am forever transformed by this experience, grateful for it and permanently dedicated to living within His kingdom.

"When we wholeheartedly dedicate our talents and abilities to serve God's purpose, our lives become a melody of worship and praise."

Rosel Joy Bona

Bibliography

Barclay, John M G. 2017. *Paul and the Gift*. Grand Rapids, Michigan: William B. Eerdmans Publishing Company.

Barlaan, Bea, Lee Simon Brown, Ann Del Rosario, and Joshua Gayanelo. 2020. "Lilim (in Your Shelter)." Http://Bit.ly/Thisisvictoryworship. Victory Worship. March 20, 2020. http://victoryworship.ph.

Batterson, Mark. 2016. *The Circle Maker*. Zondervan.

Bauckham, Richard. 1993. *The Theology of the Book of Revelation*. Cambridge: Cambridge University Press.

Bible. 1984. *The Holy Bible : King James Version*. New York: American Bible Society.

"Bible Commentary - Matthew Henry Consise." n.d. Biblestudytools.com. Accessed October 17, 2023. https://www.biblestudytools.com/commentaries/matthew-henry-concise.

Biblica. 2011. *Holy Bible : New International Version*. Authentic Bibles.

Blackaby, Henry T, Richard Blackaby, and Claude V King. 2018a. *Experiencing God : Knowing and Doing the Will of God*. Nashville, Tennessee: B & H Publishing Group.

———. 2018b. *Experiencing God : Knowing and Doing the Will of God*. Nashville, Tennessee: B & H Publishing Group.

Bounds, E.M. 2016. *The Essentials of Prayer*. Gideon House Books.

Brené Brown. 2014. *The Gifts of Imperfection : Let Go of Who You Think You're Supposed to Be and Embrace Who You Are.* Charleston, Sc: Instaread Summaries.

Brennan Manning. 1990. *The Ragamuffin Gospel : Good News for the Bedraggled, Beat-Up, and Burnt Out.* Portland, Or.: Multnomah.

———. 2015. *The Ragamuffin Gospel.* Colorado Springs, Colorado Multnomah Books.

Brennan Manning, John Blase, and Jonathan Foreman. 2015a. *Abba's Child : The Cry of the Heart for Intimate Belonging.* Colorado Springs, Co: Navpress.

———. 2015b. *Abba's Child : The Cry of the Heart for Intimate Belonging.* Colorado Springs, Co: Navpress.

Bridges, Jerry. 2016a. *The Pursuit of Holiness.* Colorado Springs, Colorado: Navpress.

———. 2016b. *Trusting God.* Colorado Springs: Navpress.

Bright, John. 2010. *The Kingdom of God.* Abingdon Press.

Brueggemann, Walter. 2014. *Sabbath as Resistance : Saying No to the Culture of Now.* Louisville, Ky: Westminster John Knox Press.

Caine, Christine. 2016. *Unashamed.* Thomas Nelson.

Calvin, Jean, John T Mcneill, and Ford Lewis Battles. 1960. *Institutes of the Christian Religion.* Philadelphia, Westminster Press.

Carson, D A. 1978. *Jesus' Sermon on the Mount : And His Confrontation with the World : An Exposition of Matthew 5-10.* Grand Rapids, Mi: Baker.

Chambers, Oswald. 2010. *My Utmost for His Highest.* Our Daily Bread Publishing.

Chan, Francis, and Danae Yankoski. 2013. *Crazy Love : Overwhelmed by a Relentless God.* Colorado Springs, Co: David C. Cook.

Charles Haddon Spurgeon. 1983. *The Treasury of David.*

Claiborne, Shane. 2010. *The Irresistible Revolution.* ReadHowYouWant.com.

Clive Staples Lewis. 1952. *Mere Christianity.* Scribner Paper Fiction.

Cloud, Henry, and John Sims Townsend. 2002. *Boundaries: When to Say Yes, How to Say No, to Take Control of Your Life.* Grand Rapids, Mich.: Zondervan Pub. House.

Corrie Ten Boom, Elizabeth Sherrill, and John L Sherrill. 2008. *The Hiding Place.* Grand Rapids, Mi: Chosen Books.

Curry, Michael B. 2018. *The Power of Love: Sermons, Reflections, and Wisdom to Uplift and Inspire.* New York, Ny: Avery.

Dietrich Bonhoeffer. 1995. *The Cost of Discipleship.* New York: Simon And Schuster.

———. (1937) 2015. *The Cost of Discipleship.* London: Scm Press.

Edwards, Jonathan. 1835. *The Works of Jonathan Edwards.*

Eldredge, John. 2010. *Walking with God.* Thomas Nelson.

———. 2011. *Wild at Heart - Discovering the Secret of a Mans Soul.* Thomas Nelson Publishers.

———. 2016a. *Waking the Dead: The Secret to a Heart Fully Alive.* Nashville, Tennessee: Nelson Books, An Imprint Of Thomas Nelson.

———. 2016b. *Walking with God.* Thomas Nelson.

Evans, Tony. 2008. *The Battle Is the Lords.* Moody Publishers.

Foster, Richard J. 2018. *Celebration of Discipline: The Path to Spiritual Growth.* San Francisco: Harperone.

France, Richard T. 2014. *The Gospel of Mark a Commentary on the Greek Text.* Grand Rapids, Mich. Eerdmans.

Frangipane, Francis. 2006. *The Three Battlegrounds.* Cedar Rapids, Ia: Arrow Publications.

Franklin, Jentezen. 2014. *Fasting: Opening the Door to a Deeper, More Intimate, More Powerful Relationship with God.* Lake Mary: Charisma House.

Garlow, James L, Gerard Reed, and John C Maxwell. 2002. *The 21 Irrefutable Laws of Leadership Tested by Time: Those Who Followed Them--and Those Who Didn't.* Nashville, Tenn.: Thomas Nelson Publishers.

Goff, Bob. 2012. *Love Does - Discover a Secretly Incredible Life in an Ordinary World.* Thomas Nelson Publishers.

Graham, Billy. 1993. *The Collected Works of Billy Graham.* New York: Inspirational Press.

———. 2011. *The Holy Spirit.* Thomas Nelson.

Groeschel, Craig. 2013. *Altar Ego.* Zondervan.

H. Nouwen. 1993. *In the Name of Jesus: Reflections on Christian Leadership.* Turtleback Books.

Henri J M Nouwen. 1979. *The Wounded Healer.* New York Doubleday (An Image Book.

———. 1986. *Reaching out : The Three Movements of the Spiritual Life.* Garden City, N.Y.: Image Books.

———. 1994. *Return of the Prodigal Son : Story of Homecoming.* Darton, L. & T.

———. 2002. *Life of the Beloved : Spiritual Living in a Secular World.* New York: Crossroad Pub. Co.

———. 2016. *The Way of the Heart : The Spirituality of the Desert Fathers and Mothers.* New York: Harperone.

Henry, Matthew. 2020. *Matthew Henry's Commentary on the Whole Bible.* Peabody, Massachusetts: Hendrickson Publishers, Llc.

Hughes, Selwyn. 2004. *Walking in His Ways.* Cwr.

Jakes, T D. 2014. *Instinct.* FaithWords.

Johnson, Bill. 2010. *When Heaven Invades Earth.* ReadHowYouWant.com.

Keener, Craig S. 2013. *Paul, Women, & Wives : Marriage and Women's Ministry in the Letters of Paul.* Grand Rapids, Mi: Baker Academic.

———. 2014. *The IVP Bible Background Commentary : New Testament.* Downers Grove, Illinois: Intervarsity Press.

Keller, Timothy. 2008. *The Reason for God : Belief in an Age of Skepticism.* New York: Dutton.

———. 2011. *Counterfeit Gods : The Empty Promises of Money, Sex, and Power, and the Only Hope That Matters*. New York: Riverhead Books.

———. 2016a. *The Prodigal God : Recovering the Heart of the Christian Faith*. New York, New York: Penguin Books.

———. 2016b. *The Reason for God: Belief in an Age of Skepticism*. New York: Penguin.

———. 2016c. *Walking with God through Pain and Suffering*. New York: Penguin Books.

———. 2018. *Making Sense of God : An Invitation to the Sceptical*. London: Hodder & Stoughton Ltd.

Keller, Timothy J. 2014. *The Freedom of Self-Forgetfulness : The Path to True Christian Joy*. Farington, Uk: 10Publishing.

Keller, Timothy, and Kathy Keller. 2013a. *The Meaning of Marriage : Facing the Complexities of Commitment with the Wisdom of God*. New York: Riverhead Books.

———. 2013b. *The Meaning of Marriage : Facing the Complexities of Commitment with the Wisdom of God*. New York: Riverhead Books.

Lamott, Anne, and Anchor Books. 2006. *Traveling Mercies : Some Thoughts on Faith*. New York: Anchor Books, [Post.

Lewis, C S. 1996. *The Joyful Christian : 127 Readings from C.S. Lewis*. New York: Touchstone Book.

———. 2009. *Mere Christianity : A Revised and Amplified Edition, with a New Introduction, of the Three Books Broadcast Talks, Christian Behaviour, and beyond Personality*. New York: Harperone.

———. 2011. *The Screwtape Letters (Enhanced Special Illustrated Edition)*. Harper Collins.

———. 2021. *Letters to Malcolm: Chiefly on Prayer*. Good Press.

Lewis, C S, and Pauline Baynes. 2009. *The Lion, the Witch and the Wardrobe. #2*. New York, Ny: Harper.

Lewis, C S, and Harpercollins Publishers. 2001. *The Weight of Glory and Other Addresses*. New York: Harperone. https://www.christianbook.com/the-weight-glory-and-other-addresses/c-s-lewis/9780060653200/pd/653205.

Lewis, C. S. (1952) 2017. *Mere Christianity*. Harpercollins Publishers.

Lewis, Clive S. 2014. *The Problem of Pain*. New York, NY: Harpercollins.

Lucado, Max. 2011a. *Cure for the Common Life*. Thomas Nelson.

———. 2011b. *It's Not about Me*. Thomas Nelson.

———. 2011c. *God's Story, Your Story*. Zondervan.

———. 2012a. *Fearless*. Thomas Nelson.

———. 2012b. *Outlive Your Life*. Thomas Nelson.

———. 2015. *You'll Get through This (Miniature Edition)*. Running Press Miniature Editions.

———. 2017. *Less Fret, More Faith*. Thomas Nelson.

———. 2019. *Anxious for Nothing : Finding Calm in a Chaotic World*. Nashville, Tennessee: Thomas Nelson.

———. 2021. *In the Grip of Grace*. S.L.: Thomas Nelson Pub.

Lucado, Max, and Amanda Haley. 2012. *Grace : More than We Deserve, Greater than We Imagine. A Participant's Guide to Small Group Study*. Nashville, Tenn.: Thomas Nelson.

Lucado, Max, and Sergio Martinez. 2007. *You Are Special*. Wheaton, Ill.: Crossway Books.

Luther, Martin. 2019. *Strength to Love*. Beacon Press.

Macarthur, John. 1984. *1 Corinthians*. Chicago: Moody Press.

———. 2008. *The Gospel according to Jesus : What Is Authentic Faith?* Grand Rapids, Mich.: Zondervan.

———. 2013. *The MacArthur Study Bible*. Nashville, Tn: Thomas Nelson.

Manning, Brennan. 1998. *Reflections for Ragamuffins*. Harper Collins.

Maxwell, John C. 2001. *The Winning Attitude ; Developing the Leaders around You ; Becoming a Person of Influence*. Nashville, Tn: T. Nelson Publishers.

———. 2008. *Today Matters*. Center Street.

Mcneill, Donald P, Douglas A Morrison, and Nouwen Henri J. M. 2005. *Compassion : A Reflection on the Christian Life*. New York: Image Books/Doubleday.

Meyer, Joyce, and Todd Hafer. 2006. *Battlefield of the Mind for Teens : Winning the Battle in Your Mind*. Faith Words.

Moore, Beth. 2007. *Breaking Free : Discover the Victory of Total Surrender*. Nashville, Tenn.: Broadman & Holman.

Moore, Beth, and Dale Mccleskey. 2013. *Jesus, the One and Only*. Nashville, Tenn.: Broadman & Holman.

Mouw, Richard J. 2010. *Uncommon Decency : Christian Civility in an Uncivil World*. Downers Grove, Illinois: Ivp Books.

Munroe, Myles. 2004. *Rediscovering the Kingdom : Ancient Hope for Our 21st Century World*. Shippensburg, Pa: Destiny Image Publishers.

———. 2006. *Understanding Your Potential : Discovering the Hidden You*. Shippensburg, Pa.: Destiny Image Publishers.

Nicholas Thomas Wright. 2008. *Surprised by Hope : Rethinking Heaven, the Resurrection, and the Mission of the Church*. New York: Harperone.

Nouwen, Henri. 2013. *The Return of the Prodigal Son : A Story of Homecoming*. The Crown Publishing Group.

Ortberg, John. 2009. *The Life You've Always Wanted*. Zondervan.

Os Guinness. 2003. *The Call : Finding and Fulfilling the Central Purpose of Your Life*. Nashville, Tenn.: Thomas Nelson.

———. 2018. *The Call : Finding and Fulfilling God's Purpose for Your Life*. Nashville, Tennessee: W Publishing Group, An Imprint Of Thomas Nelson.

Oswald Chambers, and James Reimann. 2018. *My Utmost for His Highest*. Grand Rapids, Michigan: Discovery House.

Packer J. I. (author). 2017. *Knowing God through the Year*. InterVarsity Press.

Packer, J I. 1993. *Knowing God : Study Guide*. Downers Grove, Il: Intervarsity Press.

———. 2011. *Concise Theology*. Tyndale House Publishers, Inc.

———. 2012. *Evangelism and the Sovereignty of God*. Downers Grove, Ill.: Ivp Books.

Paul, John. 2013. *Crossing the Threshold of Hope*. Knopf.

Peterson, Eugene H. 2019. *A Long Obedience in the Same Direction : Discipleship in an Instant Society*. Downers Grove: Intervarsity Press.

Pink, Terry. 2015. *Attributes of God*.

Piper, John. 2011. *Desiring God : Meditations of a Christian Hedonist*. Colorado Springs, Colo.: Multnomah.

———. 2013. *Future Grace, Revised Edition : The Purifying Power of the Promises of God*. Colorado Springs, Colo.: Multnomah Books.

———. 2017. *Desiring God : Meditations of a Christian Hedonist*. Colorado Springs, Colorado: Multnomah Books.

———. 2018a. *Don't Waste Your Life*. Wheaton, Ill.: Crossway Books.

———. 2018b. *Don't Waste Your Life (Redesign)*. Crossway.

Prince, Derek. 2003. *War in Heaven*. Chosen Books.

Prince, Joseph. 2020. *Destined to Reign Anniversary Edition*. Destiny Image Publishers.

Saint, Steve. 2005. *End of the Spear : A True Story*. Carol Stream, Ill.: Tyndale House Publishers.

Schaper, Donna. 2018. *Never Enough Time*. Rowman & Littlefield.

Shirer, Priscilla. 2017. *Discerning the Voice of God : How to Recognize When God Speaks*. Nashville, Tennessee: Lifeway Press.

Smedes, Lewis B. 1997. *The Art of Forgiving : When You Need to Forgive and Don't Know How*. New York: Ballantine Books.

Snyder, John I. 2011. *Your 100 Day Prayer*. Thomas Nelson Inc.

Sproul, R C, and Jinshen Yao. 2001. *Essential Truths of the Christian Faith /Shen Xue Ru Men = Essential Truths of the Christian Faith*. E. Brunswick, Nj: Geng Xin Zhuan Dao Hui.

Sproul, R.C. 2016. *Reason to Believe*. Zondervan Academic.

———. 2023. *The Holiness of God*. NavPress.

Spurgeon, C H. 1994. *Morning + Evening : Daily Readings.* Fearn, Ross-Shire, Scotland, Uk: Christian Focus Publications.

Spurgeon, Charles H. 2022. *Morning by Morning.* Hendrickson Publishers.

Stanley, Charles. 2008. *The Power of God's Love.* Thomas Nelson.

———. 2013. *The Charles F. Stanley Life Principles Bible, Nasb.* Nashville, Tennessee: Thomas Nelson.

Stevenson, Bryan. 2020. *JUST MERCY : A Story of Justice and Redemption.* S.L.: Scribe Publications.

Stott, John R W. 2014. *The Living Church : Convictions of a Lifelong Pastor.* Nottingham: Inter-Varsity Press.

———. 2020. *The Message of Romans : God's Good News for the World.* Downers Grove, Illinois: Ivp Academic, [] Â.

Stott, John R. W. 1988. *The Letters of John : An Introduction and Commentary.* Downers Grove, Illinois: IVP Academic.

Swindoll, Charles R. 1994. *The Finishing Touch.* Thomas Nelson.

Swindoll, Charles R, and Ken Gire. 2002. *Living above the Level of Mediocrity : A Commitment to Excellence : Insight for Living Bible Study Guide.* Plano, Tx: Insight For Living.

Teresa, Mother. 2007. *A Simple Path.* Ballantine Books.

———. 2010. *No Greater Love.* New World Library.

The Holy Bible : English Standard Version : Containing the Old and New Testaments. 2020. Wheaton, Illinois: Crossway.

Thomas, Gary. 2020. *Sacred Pathways.* Zondervan.

Thurman, Howard. 1996. *Jesus and the Disinherited.* Boston, Ma: Beacon Press.

Tolle, Eckhart. 2018. *The Power of Now : A Guide to Spiritual Enlightenment.* Sydney, Nsw: Hachette Australia.

Tozer, A W. 2004. *The Pursuit of God.* Milton Keynes, Bucks ; Waynesboro, Ga: Authentic Media.

———. 2015. *The Pursuit of God: The Human Thirst for the Divine*. Chicago: Moody Publishers.

———. 2019. *How to Be Filled with the Holy Spirit*. New Delhi: General Press.

———. 2020. *Pursuit of God*. S.L.: Bethany House.

———. 2022a. *The Knowledge of the Holy*. DigiCat.

Tozer, A W, and Hoopla Digital. 2019. *The Knowledge of the Holy: The Attributes of God, Their Meaning in the Christian Life*. United States: General Press, Made Available through Hoopla.

Tozer, A. W. 2013. *Pursuit of God*. Minneapolis, Minn.: Bethany House.

Tozer, A.W. 2022b. *The Root of the Righteous (Sea Harp Timeless Series)*. Destiny Image Publishers.

Tyndale, and Tyndale House Publishers. 2013. *Holy Bible, Giant Print NLT*. Tyndale House Publishers, Inc.

Vanzant, Iyanla. 2012. *In the Meantime: Finding Yourself and the Love You Want*. Riverside: Simon & Schuster, Limited.

Vins, Holly, Jesse Bell, Shubhayu Saha, and Jeremy Hess. 2015. "The Mental Health Outcomes of Drought: A Systematic Review and Causal Process Diagram." *International Journal of Environmental Research and Public Health* 12 (10): 13251–75. https://doi.org/10.3390/ijerph121013251.

Voskamp, Ann. 2011. *One Thousand Gifts: A Dare to Live Fully Right Where You Are*. Zondervan.

Vvolkowski, Kenneth J. 1963. "The Confessions of St. Augustine." *New Scholasticism* 37 (3): 383–84. https://doi.org/10.5840/newscholas196337329.

W Phillip Keller. 2015. *A Shepherd Looks at Psalm 23*. Grand Rapids: Zondervan.

Walsh, Sheila. 2009. *God Has a Dream for Your Life*. Thomas Nelson.

Waltke, Bruce K. 2005. *The Book of Proverbs Chapters 15 - 31*. Grand Rapids, Mich. [U.A.] Eerdmans Publ.

Warren, Rick. 2006. *The Purpose Driven Life*. Chagrin Falls, Oh: Zondervan.

———. 2008. *God's Power to Change Your Life*. Zondervan.

———. 2016. *The Purpose-Driven Life: What on Earth Am I Here For?* Grand Rapids, Mich.: Zondervan.

Watchman Nee. 2020. *Normal Christian Life*. S.L.: Value Classic Reprints.

Wiersbe, Warren W. 1995. *The Strategy of Satan : How to Detect and Defeat Him*. Carol Stream, Ill.: Tyndale House Publishers.

———. 2009. *Be Skillful : God's Guidebook to Wise Living : OT Commentary : Proverbs*. Colorado Springs, Co: David C. Cook.

———. 2010. *Be Strong (Joshua)*. David C Cook.

———. 2016. *The Bumps Are What You Climb On*. Baker Books.

Wigglesworth, Smith. 2013. *Faith That Prevails*. Simon and Schuster.

Willard, Dallas. 2018a. *The Divine Conspiracy : Rediscovering Our Hidden Life in God*. New York: Harperone.

———. 2018b. *The Divine Conspiracy : Rediscovering Our Hidden Life in God*. New York: Harperone.

Willard, Dallas, and James Bryan Smith. 2021. *Hearing God : Developing a Conversational Relationship with God*. Downers Grove, IL: InterVarsity Press.

Wright, N T. 2012. *After You Believe : Why Christian Character Matters*. New York: Harpercollins.

———. 2016. *The Day the Revolution Began*. HarperCollins.

———. 2018. *Surprised by Hope : Rethinking Heaven, the Resurrection, and the Mission of the Church*. New York: Harperone, An Imprint Of Harpercollins Publishers.

———. 2021. *Simply Christian*. London: Society For Promoting Christian Knowledge.

Wright, Tom. 2011. *Simply Christian*. Spck Publishing.

Young, Sarah. 2013. *Jesus Calling : Enjoying Peace in His Presence*. Nashville: Thomas Nelson.

———. 2022. *Jesus Calling My First Bible Storybook*. Thomas Nelson.

Zacharias, Ravi K. 2010. *The Grand Weaver : How God Shapes Us through the Events of Our Lives*. Grand Rapids, Mich.: Zondervan.

Zondervan Publishing, and Zondervan Publishing Staff. 1996. *Holy Bible*. Zondervan Publishing Company.

About the Author

Rosel Joy Bona is an individual who embodies faith, dedication, and love. He is a husband, a caring father, and an enthusiastic missionary. Rosel's mission in life revolves around inspiring and empowering people to live their lives through their unshakeable faith in God.

With compassion and a strong desire to make a positive impact, Rosel oversees two churches abroad to ensure that believers worldwide have access to spiritual guidance and support. Additionally, he annually organizes conferences for pastors and leaders in communities, equipping them with the necessary tools and knowledge to bring about lasting change in their respective areas.

However, Rosel's mission extends beyond the boundaries of the church. His goal is to reach villages in the Philippines and Africa where opportunities are scarce. Recognizing the importance of education, Rosel ensures that school supplies are provided to parents who cannot afford them. This initiative gives children in these regions the chance to dream big and thrive.

Rosel's unwavering faith in God's plans fuels his passion. He can inspire others through his speeches and writings, encouraging them to pursue their unique paths with confidence.

In his book titled "In His Kingdom ", Rosel takes readers on a journey into the realm of God's presence, vividly describing the boundlessness and incomprehensibility of His love and grace. This captivating expedition acts as a catalyst for individuals to deepen their connections with God.

Having personally witnessed the transformative power of faith and service, Rosel comprehends the impact they can have on communities worldwide. He firmly believes that when people come together with a shared purpose, remarkable transformations can take place. Thus, his mission extends beyond offering support and guidance; he also aims to reveal to others the vast possibilities that await them when they wholeheartedly dedicate their lives to serving God.

Rosel Joy Bona serves as a motivating force, igniting faith and purpose wherever he goes. Through his endeavours, commitment to education, and unwavering pursuit of God's presence, Rosel uplifts individuals and empowers them to embrace their unique callings while making a lasting impact on the world around them. His unwavering dedication to his mission serves as a reminder that by surrendering our lives to God, we open ourselves up to incredible possibilities.

www.ingramcontent.com/pod-product-compliance
Lightning Source LLC
Chambersburg PA
CBHW062032290426
44109CB00026B/2610